EVERY GOOD BOY DOES FINE

BOBBY MIGUEL LAGUNA

Gotham Books

30 N Gould St.
Ste. 20820, Sheridan, WY 82801
https://gothambooksinc.com/

Phone: 1 (307) 464-7800

© 2024 *Bobby Miguel Laguna*. All rights reserved.

No part of this book may be reproduced, stored in a retrieval system, or transmitted by any means without the written permission of the author.

Published by Gotham Books (May 9, 2024)

ISBN: 979-8-88775-827-5 (P)
ISBN: 979-8-88775-828-2 (E)

Because of the dynamic nature of the Internet, any web addresses or links contained in this book may have changed since publication and may no longer be valid.

The views expressed in this work are solely those of the author and do not necessarily reflect the views of the publisher, and the publisher hereby disclaims any responsibility for them.

DEDICATION

This book is dedicated to my wife, Nellie, and our four children, Miguel Laguna III, Robert, Steven, and Leslie. For their unconditional love and support through my journey.

TABLE OF CONTENTS

I	1
II	22
III	49
IV	59
V	78
VI	90
VII	97
VIII	110
IX	121
X	129
XI	139
XII	152
XIII	169
XIV	181
XV	197
XVI	212
XVII	226
XVIII	242
XIX	253
XX	267

I

HERE I AM AGAIN. THIS WAS the thought foremost in my mind as I sat in the waiting room of a hospital in New York City, waiting my turn to be interviewed. I was there to be admitted into the detox ward. There must have been about twenty to twenty-five other addicts doing the same.

First came an interview with a drug counselor, and then with a doctor, as each person went through the process, I could not help thinking, why am I here with these people? I could never accept myself as a hopeless addict. Maybe we were all thinking the same thing. I don't know. Things could have been so different if I had never gotten so deeply involved with drugs.

I don't know why I didn't let myself think of the future; I guess I didn't think I had a future; at that time, I had no power over my life. I knew that I didn't want to use drugs, but I had no control. Life just felt so empty without them.

Maybe not accepting my condition as hopeless was false. Was I hopeless? I was not sure. If only I didn't have to worry about it. I knew that it would be a lot easier if I accepted it. What did I have to lose? Nothing. I had already lost my self-respect. It made me feel bad that I was thinking about this so much and not coming up with any answers.

No one has an answer, I told myself. No one can help me. This program can't help, so why am I here? I should be out in the street trying to get high. I still have my works (my works means my drug paraphernalia) at home. Maybe I could find something in the house to sell. I should get up and leave.

Thinking of home caused me to think of my wife. Nellie expects me to be in this program today. When I left her this morning, she seemed to be relieved that I was leaving for a while. I really can't blame her; it must really be rough on her. Having to deal with my addiction to drugs has to be a terrible life for anyone. I'm sure she must have considered leaving me many times. I can't see why she's put up with me all these years. She was very affected by having her own parents separated. Maybe that's what has prevented her from leaving me. I better: stay here and get myself into this program. She needs a break from me. I looked around and assessed my situation.

I've been waiting here for a good two hours, and the drugs I took this morning have worn off. I can tell because I feel the funny feeling in my throat. I hope they hurry up and call me before I really get sick. I wonder who is selling some drugs out there. Maybe I could take a quick run out and get high without losing my turn. Let me see how many people are in front of me.

Suddenly I heard my name being called, and I knew I'd have to forget about getting high now. As I walked toward the office, I could see an orderly waiting to take me to the detox ward.

"I'm starting to get sick," I told them, putting my hand on my stomach and giving a little bend so he could see that I was getting some discomfort.

I sort of overdid it, but the effort was well rewarded. When he told the nurse to give me some medication to relieve my sickness, I smiled. I had figured out the system.

As soon as I finished drinking the medication, the orderly took me to a locker room where I was given a pair of pajamas and a robe. I was also given a large brown envelope for my personal property. As I emptied my pockets, I realized that I had a large knife in one of them.

I should have left it at home. I was certain they would not allow me to put it in the envelope.

I'll just try to slip it in. Maybe they won't look into it.

I took out my wallet with some other things and put them inside the envelope, and then I reached for the knife and slipped it in also. No one noticed. I sealed it up and handed it over to the attendant. So far it has not been detected.

I was also instructed to take off my clothes and put on the hospital gown. As I entered a cubicle to do so, the orderly looked in the envelope, and shouted at me,

"Hey, buddy, we aren't allowed to accept knives in here."

I gave him a blank look, not knowing what to say.

He continued. "If you want, I can get rid of it for you."

Being half-undressed and not wanting to cause any problems, I said "okay" and then finished changing.

I was escorted up to the fourteenth floor to the detox ward. As I entered, I noticed a few familiar faces. After waving a brief hello, I was taken into a room with six beds. The room was no different from those in most hospitals: three beds on one side and three on the other.

The orderly pointed to my bed and told me I could lie in it anytime I wanted. I was allowed to bring some cigarettes, soap, and toothpaste, and was thinking how briefly they had checked my belongings downstairs. I could have snuck some drugs in the toothpaste, and they wouldn't have seen it. But what the hell? That would only prolong my withdrawal.

They might even have discharged me from the hospital if they had found it or saw me looking high.

The ward was long and must have held about thirty patients.

Although it looked like any other hospital ward it did have some differences. The front door was locked, and guards were always in front of it. It had a small, makeshift dining room, and all the patients were expected to eat in it. No bedside services!

About three p.m. in the afternoon, I began feeling sick. I wondered if the medication they gave me was really drugs or if it was just a placebo. My legs were starting to bother me, the first telltale sign that I was getting sick. I tried not to think about it. From past experience, I knew that after a few days I would start getting better. I had been through detox many times, and I was always able to survive. I knew that if I stayed the thirty days required, I was going to be drug free when I left. For me, that was when the real battle started. I'd just have to stay away from drugs, and I knew it wouldn't be easy.

I looked at other people, and they seemed to have so much more control. For them, life should be less difficult.

I remember back to when I took that first shot of heroin and how it seemed so harmless. It was so easy to convince myself that I wouldn't get hooked again. It seemed to me that people should be able to have that kind of control.

My mind continued to question the whole drug scene. What is it about this drug that has so completely ruled my life? Why is it that I have to be one of those people who are caught up on this continuous merry-go-round?

I could hear people moving about in the hallway. As I looked toward the door, I could see a few patients walking in the direction of the medication. My legs were really giving me trouble, and I was starting to feel some aches and pains all over my body.

I walked out of my room and found a place in line. I wondered how many people were in front of me. As I leaned over to count, I felt someone pull on my robe. I turned and noticed that the person pulling my robe was an old friend of mine whom I hadn't seen in a couple of years. His name was on the tip of my tongue. I remembered doing time with him in Elmira, where I first met him. After we both got out, I saw him a few times in Spanish Harlem. I had gone to 109th Street to buy drugs and met up with him there. He was already strung out. After I bought some dope, he took me to a vacant house on Lexington Avenue and we both got high. At that point, I remembered his name: Edgar.

By now I had reached the medication office, and it was my turn to get the medication that I so badly needed.

"What is your name, Sir?" the nurse asked.

When I told her, she began looking for my medication. "I'm sorry but I don't see anything here for you. If you'll just step aside until I give the others their medication, I'll call the doctor and check on it."

"Miss, I ain't feeling so good. Can't you call the doctor right now?" I asked.

She gave me a cold look. "Please step aside so I can take care of the others," she said emphasizing the word please.

I immediately moved aside, not wanting to aggravate her to the point of delaying my medication. I waited for what seemed a long time, but in actuality was only about fifteen minutes. Having been through this before, I knew that when a person was detoxing and the body was going through a lot of changes, time just seemed to stand still.

Finally, the nurse called me over and once again asked my name. I told her, then quickly asked her "How long will it be before the doctor gets here" I was feeling certain I could not wait much longer.

Without looking at me, she answered, "He's on his way."

"Thank you." I said, and then I walked down a couple of doors and stood in the hallway so I could see that front door. I really needed that medication- now! But by the tone of that nurse's voice, I could sense that she was a tough old girl and giving her a hard time was not going to work in my favor.

By that time my nose was running, and my legs were driving me crazy. It was always better to walk when my legs bothered me, so I started walking up and down the hall. I saw Edgar coming toward me.

As he got close to me, I could see he had a concerned look on his face.

"Man, you look terrible. You still haven't gotten any medication?"

Before I could answer, I heard the front door open; it was the doctor.

He walked in and went directly into the nurses' station. I didn't want to seem overly anxious, so I stayed where I was. I could hear him talking with the nurse.

It won't be long now. I was thinking, all he has to do is look at me and he will know how sick I am. Then I'll get some medication.

Then the thought hit me, what if he's one of those cold-blooded young interns? Maybe he won't give me anything at all!

The medication I had drunk earlier in the day must have been weak. It had been about five hours since they had given it to me, but already my throat felt as if something was stuck in it. The feeling made me nauseous. I felt as if an earthquake was going on in my stomach.

Then I began to think. "I'll bet that the medication they gave me earlier was a dummy." I just couldn't take the feeling in my legs.

As I leaned back on the wall, I heard Edgar's voice telling me to go down to the nurses' office. I clutched my stomach and could feel my legs buckle as I tried to stand.

Once again, I heard Edgar's voice as he walked toward me with the nurse. I glanced up and saw the nurse, the doctor, and Edgar standing over me. Through half-opened lids, I looked at the doctor and muttered,

"Something's wrong, Doc. I've never felt so bad before" I started to get up on my feet, and when I couldn't, the doctor and Edgar helped me. On our way down the hall, we stopped at a door in front of the nurses' office. The nurse opened it with a key, and I assumed the room inside was the examining room. When the door swung open, I saw I was right.

"Can you tell me how you feel?" the doctor asked once I was seated at the end of the examination table.

I started to explain, and at the same time he reached for a flashlight from his pocket and began looking at the pupils of my eyes.

I could hear the nurse thank Edgar for his help, and out of the corner of my eye saw her lead him to the door. Once it was closed, she brought over a machine to take my blood pressure.

By that time the doctor had finished and asked me to remove my pajama top. Then he started to push his fingers into the upper part of my stomach, just below the rib cage. He pressed so hard that I reached for his hand. Before I could complain, he pulled his hand back. I could see that whatever he was looking for, he found. He called the nurse to the side. I could not hear what he was telling her, but whatever it was, it seemed very serious.

The nurse stepped out of the examination room, and at the same time, the doctor went over to a cabinet and pulled out a surgical mask. He placed it on his face, and then came over to me.

"How have you been feeling lately?" he asked. "Have you noticed anything out of the ordinary?"

"I really haven't given it much thought," I told him, "but now that I think about it, I have been waking up at night drenched in sweat, I've also noticed that my urine has been darker than usual."

By the look on the doctor's face, I could see that I was confirming what he had already been suspecting.

Just then the nurse entered the examination room and handed me a small cup of methadone mixed with orange juice. I accepted it and immediately drank it down.

The doctor turned to the nurse. "Be sure that you put him in a room by himself."

The nurse nodded and wrote something on a medical chart.

When the doctor had finished making his own notes he once again looked into my eyes with his flashlight.

"How are you feeling now?" he asked.

"I feel a little better," I said. "My habit must have been stronger than I had suspected, or maybe it's an additional problem."

"Well," said the doctor, "I'm not one hundred percent sure yet, but I suspect that you have contracted hepatitis. You have all the symptoms.

That's the reason I put on this mask. If you do have hepatitis, it is a highly contagious disease. I told the nurse that you must be put in a room by yourself. I want you to seriously think about your condition.

The only way you are going to get better is to have plenty of rest. I'll see you in the morning and run some more tests to be positive."

The nurse entered the room and said 'you can put on your top now, Mr. Laguna. Then I'd like you to come with me."

I could see that she had already collected my personal belongings.

As I left the room, she handed me my bag. "Would you look in here and make sure that all your things are in it. We don't want to lose anything."

As I walked, I could feel that the medication had already made me feel better. I could feel the strength in my legs now, and the discomfort in my throat had almost disappeared. I was even walking pretty well.

Methadone is an amazing drug, I said to myself. A little more than a half hour ago I couldn't even walk on my own.

I wondered how many milligrams they had given me.

When the nurse used her key to open the door that led to the ward exit, I asked, "Where are you taking me?"

"You can't be in isolation in the drug ward. We'll have to put you in a regular hospital ward because of the hepatitis. I'm taking you down to the fourth floor."

I became concerned. "The doctor wants to see me in the morning." I told her.

"Don't worry," she assured me, "he'll know where to find you." As we entered the ward, I noticed that the door was not locked. She just pushed the door open and in we went. Walking through the corridor, I immediately had an altogether different kind of feeling. I saw people in wheelchairs; others were in bed being fed through tubes.

Suddenly I realized I had not been in a hospital since I was a little boy, and I didn't even remember that. I had my tonsils removed when I was about two or three.

I suddenly felt the impact of what it must be like being sick. I'd been addicted to drugs for about seven years and had been to quite a few programs. Many of the programs were in hospitals, but that was a whole different world. Now I was here in a hospital with people who were truly ill. It was not what I was used to.

In the past I was always sure that I could kick the habit. I never had any fear. It was always basically the same routine: after the first three days, I could be sure that I would feel better each day; after a week I would be sleeping like a baby and eating like a horse. Now this was very different. I was not prepared for this. I was not so sure I liked this at all.

I had to call my wife. I needed to talk to someone—and right away.

"I don't know anyone here," I told myself. I can't relate to these people. I looked around. I imagined some of these people would die right there. I'll probably see them being removed after they die.

Fright was creeping up on me.

The nurse appeared and took me to a room with only two beds. I was informed that I would be the only occupant. I was also told that I must stay in bed as much as possible. The room had its own toilet, and I was to use that.

When she left, saw her hang a sign on the door that read: "Isolation."

Before she shut the door, she turned and said, "It's important that this door stay closed at all times."

I suddenly realized that I was alone. I had never felt so alone in my life. I thought back to what the doctor had told me when he was examining me. I should think more seriously about my condition. I looked around the room and walked over to the window.

It was a very cloudy night and looked as if it were about to start snowing. It only served to make me feel more depressed. I wondered if the nurse would let me use the phone to call my wife. I looked at the bed and it seemed to be inviting me in. It would be good to just lie down for a while. I'd been through a lot that day and decided I might as well start getting all the rest I could.

I lay down and noticed how relaxed I felt. They must have given me a high dose of methadone, probably because of the hepatitis. I also realized that I had missed dinner. I estimated it to be around seven p.m. the door to my room had a big glass pane, and I noticed that some of the other patients looked in as they were going by. I guessed they must have been wondering why my room was isolated from the others. Seeing the expressions on their faces made me feel ashamed and angry. They could be imagining all sorts of things. I spotted the curtain around my bed and reached out and pulled it so I could hide from their view. I could not stop them from looking in, but now they could not see me and I could not see them.

I closed my eyes and started thinking how my life could be so different if I didn't have to use drugs.

Time after time I had asked myself, "Why can't I control my life? Why is it that drugs have such a hold on me?"

I wanted to stop. That was the one great thing I wanted to do. I was not happy using drugs. In fact, I was probably better off dead. I didn't want to kill myself, but sometimes I wished I had the nerve to do it. Sometimes I thought about putting a large amount of heroin in the syringe and taking it into my vein. I would die, and in time people would adjust and go on with their lives.

I started to think about it. My wife is still young, and although we have three children, she's still very attractive. She won't have any problem finding someone else. She's put up with me for so many years. It's a wonder she hasn't gotten rid me. That's something she simply lives with. I'm sure that leaving me has crossed her mind: many times.

It was not a topic that I looked forward to, so I decided to leave it alone. However, there was just one comment that she made to a close friend of hers a couple of years back that I could not forget. She must have been talking about my addiction to a friend, and from another room I heard her say she knew someday I was going to stop using drugs.

She never repeated that statement to me, and I could not understand what it was that made her believe that. If I had anything to feel good about, it was hearing someone say that about me. Someone had some faith in me.

The next thing I felt was someone tapping me on the shoulder. I opened my eyes and saw a nurse looking down at me.

"How do you feel?" she asked.

"I don't feel good at all. My pajamas are soaked with sweat."

She put a thermometer in my mouth and took my pulse. When she removed the thermometer. I asked, "What does it read?"

"One hundred and three," she said coldly, as if I were asking her something that was not my business. "Here, drink this." She handed me a cup with the methadone and orange juice along with some other medication.

"What are these pills?" I asked.

"You don't have to take them if you don't want them.

Having gone through detox so many times, I knew they were for sleeping. I emptied the cup with the pills in my mouth and swallowed them down with the methadone.

She had her face covered with a surgical mask, and all I could see was her eyes, but if eyes could kill, I would not have to worry about having hepatitis.

As she headed out of the room pushing her little medication cart, I asked her what time was.

"It's ten forty-five p.m., and I hope you don't think that you're going to get out of bed. You people are all the same. I don't know why they sent you down here."

As she left the room, she turned out the light and informed me not to cover her view with the curtain. Then she disappeared.

I felt relieved that she was gone. I got up to use the toilet. The floor felt cold, and since I didn't have slippers, I looked for my shoes. I didn't put my feet fully into them but sort of dragged them the few steps to the toilet.

Looking down, I was shocked to see that my urine had gotten really dark. It looked the color of red wine. I had heard from people that had this sickness and knew this was what happens. I also noticed in the mirror that my eyes and skin had a yellowish color. This again was the result of having hepatitis.

"I don't think the doctor is going to have much trouble deciding what I have," I half joked to myself.

I flushed the bowl, turned off the light and felt the sleeping pills taking hold of me. I started thinking of my wife and kids and wondering what they were doing right now. I removed the heavy blanket from the bed and decided to cover myself with only the sheet. I wondered why hospital beds were made up so tight. I got in the bed, and it was not long before I started to feel overcome by sleep.

Before I dozed off, I had one final thought: Please, God, help me stop using drugs.

II

MANY YEARS HAVE PASSED SINCE I first discovered I had hepatitis. I am now fifty years of age and the Executive Director of Crossroads, Inc., a bilingual program for drug rehabilitation. I have held this position for the last twelve years. As you can see, I survived that period in my life. My addiction to heroin lasted nine years. Every day was a struggle to survive. Every day was similar in the torment that I had to endure. For those nine years I could not stop myself.

I wanted desperately to stop, and I was willing to try any means I would like to tell you what some of those attempts were like.

In order to do this, we must first go back in time to May 1, 1935, when I was born. Please consider that many years have lapsed since that time, but I will describe those years as best as my memory will allow.

I was born May 1, 1935. The second child born to Librada Colon and Miguel Laguna, Sr. Being the first son, I was named after my father. My sister Aida was two and a half years older than I was. My sister Lydia and my brother Gilberto followed in that order.

The first place I remember living was on 103rd Street between Second and Third Avenue in Manhattan, New York. Only a few events stand out in my mind during that time. The death of my grandfather is one. The wake was at home, a practice that was probably common at the time. The front room was cleared of all furniture and turned into a funeral parlor. I remember him as a really good person. I think he lived with us for a short time before his death.

At that time, life and death were events that took place in the home more than now. When my brother was born, it was also in that same apartment. Once again, a room was transformed to accommodate the birth of my brother. My sisters and I were in the living room as he was entering the world.

I also remembered my first day in school. I almost drove my mother crazy because I wanted to have a notebook and pencil. She tried her best to convince me that I didn't need a notebook and pencil in kindergarten, but I wouldn't hear of it. She finally gave in and bought them for me. Needless to say, I was the only one in class who had a notebook and pencil.

I will never forget the time that I went out with my second cousin Alberto to go joyriding on the subways. It was very rare that I was allowed to go out to play, and then my mother would always be watching me from the window. She must have been distracted when Alberto walked by and took me with him. We crossed Third Avenue. We were gone for hours, and when we were on our way home, it was already dark. We were both scared when we went into my house. We just knew we were in trouble.

As we walked through the door, everyone came toward us. Alberto's mother and father went for him. My mother had me by the arm and kept asking me where I had gone. I tried to explain that it wasn't my fault. I pointed at Alberto and told them that he was the one who took me.

His mother was already beating on him. And when she heard what I said, she beat him even more. He was a lot older than I was, so he was getting all the blame.

By now his mother was dragging him by the legs into the kitchen. His father took over while she lit the oven. Pots and pans were bouncing all over the place. She said she was going to fix him so he would never go wandering off again. Each of them had him by a leg, and he was hollering and wiggling and trying to grab anything he could get his hands on. I thought they were going to stuff him in the oven.

Alberto was yelling, "I'm sorry! I'm sorry!" but no one was paying attention to him.

His shoes were off, and they were pushing his feet closer and closer to the oven. They asked him to promise never to do that again.

He wasted no time in responding with, "Yes, yes, I promise!" At that moment they let him go, and he immediately grabbed his feet. His mother looked at me and said, "How about you? Do you promise?"

I said yes even faster than he did.

After a while, Alberto's mother put her arms around him and said she was sorry, but that she did it to teach him a lesson.

As they were all leaving Alberto came over to me and in a low voice, said, "The next time I catch you alone, I'm going to kill you."

I remember moving out of 103rd Street and up to the Bronx. It had to be in 1941, because it was the same year the Second World War broke out. The news came on the radio and men were selling newspapers in the street yelling at the top of their voices about the war. Times were really rough then, but it didn't matter to me. I was too young to realize what war really was. Then my father was called down by the draft board. It appeared that they were going to take him into the army. My mother became hysterical, but later when she became calmer, she asked us all to pray.

I didn't want my father to go away, so that night I got on my knees and asked God not to let him get drafted. I don't know why I thought I had to give God a reason, but I tried to think of one. The only thing I could come up with was my father's toe. Something must have fallen on it at some time because it didn't have much of a toenail on it. He never did tell me what had happened to it. It was the only abnormal thing I could think of, so I asked God to let them see his toe.

We were all upset the day that my father went down to take his physical. When he returned to the house, however, the first thing he yelled out was that the draft board had turned him down. We were all very happy that he wasn't going off to war.

Later I heard my father tell my mother that he had been reclassified 4F because of his toe. My mother had been listening to me the night that I prayed. She knew I had mentioned his toe.

Things were bad in those days, and money was not easy to come by, so I had to learn how to hustle money at a young age. When I reached about ten years old, I started to go out shining shoes on weekends. My dad made me a shoeshine box and bought me the supplies I needed. I would always give the money I made to my mother. She would use it to buy extra things for me and my sisters and brother.

During the week I would go to the supermarket and carry groceries for people or go down to Times Square and help people with luggage. By the time I was twelve, I knew how to travel all of New York City except for Brooklyn.

School was not very exciting for me. I never did well, and I was always getting into some kind of trouble. My mother would forever be going to school at the request of my teachers. I would get into fights, skip classes, or just not do my work. I just didn't feel that I fit in. I don't know the reason for that; maybe it was a fear of being rejected.

I do remember one time when I got involved in a class talent show. We had about a week to prepare for it. I had made a request to sing a song. Other kids were also going to sing, dance, and do other things they considered themselves good at. The song I was going to sing was called "To each his own." Well, let me tell you, I practiced all week long. I just kept singing the song over and over.

On the night before the talent show, I sang the song to my mom and dad. My dad complimented me on how well I sang. My mom said that she didn't know how anyone was going to do better than me.

I was really anxious to get to school the next day. I had my mother iron my best shirt and pants that morning. When I got to school, the teacher even complimented me on how nice I looked. I was on my best behavior that day. When it was lunchtime, I took care not to mess up my clothes. No running around in the schoolyard for me that day. I stayed alone, practicing my song. (To this day I haven't forgotten the words.)

When lunch was over, we were all returning back to the classroom. I felt very special. I kept checking myself to be sure everything was in order. I was always one of the shortest kids in my class and was usually the second or third in line. The teacher would walk in the rear so she could keep an eye on all the kids.

While walking to the classroom, I noticed that one of my shoelaces had become untied. I waiting for the class to stop so I could bend down and tie it. As always, we stopped in front of our classroom. Once we were stopped, the teacher would then walk up and open the door for us to go in. That's when I bent down to tie my shoe. One of the boys took that opportunity to push the kid behind me over the top of me. I really shouldn't have gotten so mad about it, because the kids always played games like that. Any other day would have been okay to play like that, but not that day. As the kid fell over me, I lost my balance and fell down with him. My knees hit the floor hard. All the kids were laughing, and ordinarily I would have been laughing along with them. I looked at my pants and saw a hole on one of the knees.

As the teacher passes us, she told us to behave and then proceeded to open the door to the classroom. Just then I got up from the floor, really angry because of the hole in my pants. I pushed the kid who had started the whole thing. We started fighting right there in the hall. The teacher separated us and asked who had started the fight. When she found out I had started it, she took me a few doors down to the principal's office.

After she spoke with the principal, she returned to the classroom and I sat outside the office, waiting for the principal to call me inside. I waited and waited. While waiting, I could hear the kids from my classroom singing and laughing. I wasn't going to sing in front of the class. I had rehearsed that song all week, and now I wouldn't have the opportunity to sing.

When I got home, that was all I could think about. I don't even remember what the principal said to me. My mom and dad asked me how I did in school. I lied to them by telling them that the song had been a big hit. I even told them the teacher had said I was the best singer in the class. How could I have told them what really happened?

I managed to go through elementary school without being left back and went on to P.S. 52. It was a junior high school, and things didn't change much; I was still getting into all sorts of trouble.

My sister Aida did well in school and always managed to get high grades. I guess it would have been normal for me to be jealous of her, but I wasn't. As a matter-of-fact, I used to brag to my friends about how smart she was. If I was jealous, I either don't remember or it wasn't very much.

I was very protective of my sisters, but I must have driven them crazy, especially my younger sister Lydia. I never let her talk to any boys. If she went down in front of the house, I would immediately send her upstairs. I'm sure I made her life miserable.

I managed to get passing grades in junior high, but my behavior continued to get worse. I completed the ninth grade and went on to high school to become an auto mechanic; at least, that was my mother's wish. I hated it. The only period I enjoyed was machine shop. I always finished my projects faster and better than the rest of the class. As a result, the teacher had me help the other kids. I was in the machine shop for only six months, and then was moved into the auto shop.

I tried to get into it, but I just couldn't. Becoming an auto mechanic just was not going to happen. I started to cut classes and then just stopped going to school altogether. I wasn't old enough to quit school and knew this was going to bring a lot of trouble.

It was 1949 then, and drugs were fast becoming popular in the streets. I hadn't gotten into it yet, but I did smoke pot sometimes and drank wine with my friends.

One day in the late summer of that year, I left my house at about seven o'clock in the evening and headed for Union Avenue and 156th Street. This was where my club, the Lancers, hung out. We had three major interests: girls, stickball, and dancing. At that time, we were not very interested in gang fighting, although at times we found ourselves having to back away from confrontations with other gangs. It usually happened when we went to dances that were outside our neighborhood. I remember clearly how angry I would become when we would have to leave a dance in order to avoid getting into a fight with other gangs.

As I reached Union Avenue, I saw a few of the fellows standing outside the candy store. I briefly greeted everyone and asked what was happening. They readily informed me that the P.A.L. was having a dance, something to do with the summer ending.

Most of the fellows and some of the girls had arrived; however, I was still looking for one more to show up. His name was Snazzy, and he was my best friend. The club consisted of about twenty members, but as in all groups, there were a few that I grew closer to, sort of an inner group that, in our case, consisted of about six members. (I will refer to them only by their nicknames and only when it is necessary to do so.)

When the group decided to leave for the dance, I was still waiting for Snazzy.

"You guys go on ahead," I told them. "I'll wait here for Snazzy and see you later at the dance."

About a half hour later, when my patience was just about to run out, Snazzy showed up.

"Hey man, aren't you going to the P.A.L dance?" he asked.

"I've only been waiting here for about a half hour for you so we can go together," I said, half complaining. "You got any change so we can get us a bottle of wine?"

"Nope. Not tonight. I got something better in mind for us," Snazzy said, his eyes twinkling.

Assuming that he had some pot, I said "All right."

On our way to the P.A.L., Snazzy said, "Let's go to the school yard of old P.S 52 before we go to the dance."

Again, I agreed, assuming we were going there to smoke the pot. We had gone there many times in the past because it was a good place to smoke. There, one always had plenty of time to get rid of the pot in case the police came in the schoolyard.

As we reached the rear of the schoolyard, Snazzy pulled out a carefully wrapped tissue from his shirt pocket. He opened it, and I observed a small white capsule right in the center of the tissue.

He looked at me with a big smile on his face. "You want to try some of this?"

Although I had never used heroin capsules, I had seen them several times before. A couple of years back before I started to hang out around Union Avenue, I used to see the pushers on Longwood Avenue and Dawson Street selling, and even shooting, heroin. I knew that heroin was addictive.

I saw Snazzy empty the contents of the capsule on the outside of a pack of cigarettes. He then tore off the piece of a matchbook cover and made a small scoop out of it. As he was chopping up the heroin, he told me if I wanted some, I had to give him fifty cents because the capsule had cost him a dollar. I really knew I shouldn't get involved with this, but I will admit that I was a bit curious about it. Also, I didn't want Snazzy to think I was not down.

He put a scoopful up to his nose, and with his other hand, covered the other nostril. With one quick sniff, the heroin disappeared from the scoop. He repeated the procedure in the other nostril and then held out the scoop so I could do the same. I imitated what he had done, and after the second sniff, I felt a bitter taste in the back of my throat. It was a terrible taste that I had never had before. I held a blank expression on my face so that Snazzy would not notice.

As he finished the remaining half scoop, I could no longer hold back from reacting. I turned away and spit out as much as I could. I still had the taste in my mouth as we were leaving the schoolyard, but it was not as bad.

Snazzy reminded me of the half dollar I owed him. I reached in my pocket and gave him two quarters, and at the same time, I said, "Don't ever give me any of that shit again"

As we entered the P.A.L., I started to feel the reaction of the drug. It was not what I had expected. I was upset with myself for getting in this condition. I had to throw up a few times. My friends kept asking me what was wrong. I told them I was sick, and I was going to leave. I didn't even want to talk to anyone.

As I was walking out, I saw Snazzy and wondered how he was feeling. He didn't look so good; maybe he was feeling as bad as I was... I didn't know. I didn't even care.

I left the dance, and I don't remember if I went straight home or what. The thing on my mind was how sorry I was for allowing myself to get high on heroin. How could people use a drug that made you feel like this? I resolved never to use heroin again.

Four years went by before I remember using heroin again. I'm not sure if in that four-year period I tried it or not. It might have been a story I told while I was doing time in Coxsackie. I've found that sometimes when a story is told over so many times, after a few years it becomes hard to separate it from the truth. When I was doing time, I had to tell many such stories. Although I remembered most of the lies, I had to tell, I might have believed a few. Anyway, as hard as I try to remember, I don't recall having used heroin again until 1954.

In those four years, a number of major events took place in my life. One was that I was starting to express a lot of anger. To this day I cannot understand what was going on with me to cause this change. That was also the same year I met Nellie.

I remember the first day we met. I went to a birthday party, and she was there. We were not overly interested in each other at first; at least, I know she was not very impressed with me. I found out that she was not going with anyone at the time, so I asked her to dance a couple of times. I gave her my usual spiel but didn't think I was getting anywhere. The party ended, and since we were having our last dance, I gave her a light kiss on her cheek and told her I would like to see her again. I don't remember her giving me a sure answer. I left the party, and that was as much as I can recollect.

A few days later, I ran into her cousin. I asked her about Nellie, and she told me that she was fine. I suggested that she invite her to come around. She said she would and left it at that. I must have really liked the way she carried herself. The way she walked and the way she talked gave me the feeling that she was sure of herself.

Don't get me wrong. I didn't fall head over heels in love, nor was this a case of love at first sight. I just liked her and found myself thinking of her. I wanted to see her again. I wondered if she was thinking about me. Probably not, I decided. If she had wanted to see me again, she would have found a way.

Then I rationalized with, "she might have a strict family and maybe they don't allow her to go out much. When I see her cousin, I'm going to ask her."

Another week went by, and I still was unable to see her, but today I felt lucky. I had already been considering going to where she lived and waiting for her when she came home from school. But that was something a guy didn't do. It would show that I was going out of my way to see her. (As I think about it now, I guess that game hasn't changed much. It seems to me that that's still done with youngsters.)

It usually took me about fifteen minutes to walk from my house to Union Avenue where I hung out. I reached the candy store, and just as I was going to enter, I looked up the street and saw Nellie and her cousin coming down the street in the direction of the store. I went in and immediately looked for a place to sit down. I wanted to look cool when she walked in.

My friend Lefty walked over to me, and we were just starting a conversation when the door opened, and the two girls entered. Her cousin was leading her toward our direction, but they were intercepted by Snazzy and Cookie. This was a little upsetting because I remember that a couple of other guys at the dance had expressed interest in her. I maintained a straight uninterested expression on my face, but inside I was upset and getting close to the point of blowing my cool.

I was sitting on one of those stools that spins around, so I turned on the stool, I stopped when I was facing in their direction. Snazzy and Cookie were standing with their backs toward me, and I could see Nellie as I looked right between them. She had on a long grey coat and seemed to look prettier than she did the night I met her at the dance.

As she turned her face and glanced in my direction, I gave her my best smile (not too strong, but enough to get a response). She looked at me for what seemed a long time and finally smiled back. At that moment, all the anger I was feeling left me completely.

I don't think I am much of a romantic, but as I am writing and remembering, I want you, the reader, to try to feel what I felt at that particular moment. It was as though everything and everybody had disappeared from the candy store. I wonder now if it was that way with her. I never told her this in all our years together. When she reads this book, it will be the first time she will know that was to be the beginning of a relationship that would last thirty-four years (and still counting). Little did we realize what our future held. I was fifteen years old, and she was fourteen. It was ridiculous to think that two people that young could begin a serious relationship. I believe that even now.

There was an added factor we did not realize at the time: As two individuals, certain events had taken place in our lives which made us cling to each other, out of desperation more than anything else. Now, with the passage of time, I am aware of her past pain and suffering and can understand what her childhood was like. I can also see why things happened the way they did. (I sometimes have thoughts that seem crazy, but if I had created the human race, I would have had people born old and then grow younger as they got older. It would have solved a lot of problems that teenagers and young people have. Great minds in young bodies. It seems like a good idea, but I am sure it would have its drawbacks . . . Or would it?)

As months went by, we grew even closer to each other. She gave me the feeling that she needed me. Although I did not understand it then, I was hungry to feel needed.

I had started to work in the garment district in New York earning seventy-five cents an hour, which in 1951 was the minimum wage. I worked for a company that made belts for women's dresses. When I was not out delivering, I had to operate a machine that stapled the buckles on the belts.

The summer was in full bloom, and this was the first time I had to work full-time in a factory. Most of my friends were enjoying their summer vacations, and I was stuck in a hot sweatshop stapling women's belts. It was torture having to wait for it to be five o'clock so I could go home.

Taking the subway back and forth was another daily challenge that required skill and courage. People never smiled in the subways of New York, and I was beginning to understand why. Having to ride those subways every day was nothing to smile about. It must have been exceptionally hard on women. The things I saw happen to them were incredible. But that is an entirely different story.

When I got home each day, Nellie would be waiting for me. After I got cleaned up and ate, we would go up to Union Avenue and hang out. From there I would walk her home. I usually did not stay out late because I had to get up early to go to work. By the time I had been working for about three weeks, I began hating the job more and more every day. My mother would struggle with me every morning so I would not be late. She was still upset with me for leaving school so I could not do too much complaining to her.

On one particular day, I drank a cup of coffee and set out on my way to work. As I was walking the two blocks up Longwood Avenue to catch the subway, I decided I was going to take the day off. It was an exceptionally beautiful day, and I could not bring myself to get on the train. I could not go back home, either, because I would hear it from my mother.

I wandered over to Union Avenue, but it was too early in the morning, and no one was around. I wondered how I could get in contact with Nellie. I figured I would kill time until about ten o'clock and then call her cousin. Since she lived next door, she could let Nellie know I was there. We had been going out together for about six months, and our relationship was growing closer and closer as time went by. I was looking forward to seeing her again.

I sat outside the candy store for about an hour. I was thinking how nice the day was and how it would have been in that belt factory. I knew right then that I was not going to work there anymore. I wondered if working was always going to be like that. School didn't seem so bad now. Maybe I could go back in the fall. At least I could enjoy what was left of the summer.

It was just about time for me to call up Nellie's cousin. As I got up to go into the candy store, I heard someone call me. I turned and saw Lefty.

I waved at him and yelled, "I'm going to make a phone call, and then I'll be right with you."

When I entered the phone booth, I noticed he was headed in the direction of the candy store. I dialed the number and waited for someone to answer. Nellie's cousin answered the phone.

"Hi," I said. "Could you call Nellie to the phone?"

"Wait just a minute," she answered, and I could hear her set the receiver down and call Nellie.

While I was waiting, I opened the door to the phone booth to talk to Lefty.

"What are you doing here?" he asked. "How come you're not at work?"

"I'm fed up with that dumb job. I'm going to quit."

A short exchange of words with Lefty followed, but I was cut short when I heard Nellie on the phone. After the obvious question was asked, I repeated the same answer I gave Lefty.

"Can you come out and see me?" I asked eagerly.

"I've got some things to do around the house first. I can meet you at noon, if that's okay."

"Great. I'll wait for you in the candy store on Union Avenue."

After hanging up the phone, I continued my conversation with Lefty. He was telling me how some of the fellows were occasionally hanging out around Washington Heights. There was a club called the Dragons that hung out in that section of New York. They were growing in numbers and trying to establish a reputation. He told me how some of the guys in our inner group were thinking of joining the Dragons. I could sense that he was trying to get me interested. I must admit that I was; I wanted to hear more about the Dragons.

Lefty spent the better part of an hour telling me what had happened so far, and he somehow seemed to be seeking my approval. For me to approve of joining the Dragons was important to the group. Even though the Lancers were not known as a fighting gang, I had been elected as the war counselor, the only member of the club who could officially call a fight with another gang. Actually, it was somewhat frustrating holding this position because the lancers never fought another gang.

(It was sort of like being the Maytag repairman on today's TV commercials.)

Lefty kept explaining, and I kept asking questions until Nellie arrived. After changing the conversation, the three of us talked and joked a little while. We walked out of the candy store, and Lefty went one way and Nellie, and I went the other.

Nellie wanted to know more about why I was going to quit the job. I told her how I just couldn't stand doing that type of work. While giving her this explanation, I was getting some bad feelings about myself. I wondered if this was the way it was going to be with whatever job I had. I knew that everyone had to work in order to function in society. What if I wasn't capable of maintaining a job? I was already feeling bad about myself; this was only making me feel worse.

We walked for a while, and before we knew it, we were close to St. Mary's park. It was such a beautiful day, and we seemed to be drawn in by the trees and grass. We sat on the grass and talked for a long time. Getting into the mood of the situation, we were able to share our feelings with each other. We talked about getting married so we could be together all the time. I was sixteen then, and she was a year younger. I had heard somewhere that people could get married in New Jersey at sixteen years of age. I didn't even know if it was true. I am sure that we both wanted to believe it. The summer went by, and in September we both went back to school. This time I made a serious attempt to finish high school. I kept reminding myself of that belt factory and how I would hate to have an experience like that again. But I had no interest in school, and every day was worse than the one before. A month went by, and I found that I could not take it anymore. I finally quit, and this time I would never go back.

Once again, I went to the garment district and found a job in a dress factory. This job was not as bad as the one I held during the summer. This time I was out delivering dresses most of the time, and I liked that a lot better. However, that subway never changed.

I didn't work there very long. My aunt's husband was able to get me a better job in a machine shop. He was a tool and die maker, and a good one at that. I had told him that I knew how to operate a number of different machines and showed him some of the projects I had made in school. He seemed impressed, and that was how I got the job. I was now making one dollar an hour, and it wasn't very long before I was given an increase of fifteen cents an hour. I couldn't believe how well I was doing and how much I liked this job. I was also learning a trade.

I was a different person when I was on the job. My life away from work was now starting to get a bit more complicated. I found myself hanging out on the West Side with the Dragons, and I had to divide my time between Nellie and the guys.

I should have known my life was headed in the wrong direction.

III

BEING A MEMBER OF THE DRAGONS was very different than belonging to the Lancers. The Lancers were more of a club; the Dragons were a gang. When you were a member of a gang like the Dragons, you didn't back out of fights. I was trying to establish a reputation in the gang. I would start fights because I knew I had the support of the others. When I went to parties, I would usually start a big fight and end the party. It was all so crazy. I was becoming a walking time bomb. It was getting to the point that whenever any of the gang members had any trouble, they would wait for me before any action was taken.

The cold weather was starting to set in and cut into a lot of the hanging around. I had been spending more time with the gang and less time with Nellie. I wanted to keep my relationship with Nellie more private and away from that whole scene and would only see her whenever I did not go to the West Side. I wouldn't take her with me, and she wasn't too happy about that. We would argue about it, and after we argued, I would stay with her a couple of days. Then I would not see her for many weeks. She continued to protest, and the same procedure would once again be repeated. Gradually I was starting to spend more time with Nellie and less time with the gang. Fall and early winter went like that. Maybe it was the cold weather, or possibly I was just loosing interest in the gang. I do recall that we were together a lot during the Christmas holidays.

1952 started out real good for me. I was still working in the machine shop, and Nellie and I were closer than ever. I would seldom go hang around with the guys. It remained like that for the rest of the winter. I turned seventeen in May, and Nellie sixteen in June. We were as close as two people could get. We even started talking about marriage again.

This time we were being more realistic about it. We no longer planned to run away to New Jersey. Nellie still had two years left before she finished high school. It seemed to us that we could wait till then. I guess we could say that it was bad timing, but those plans had to change.

It must have been about the middle of June when Nellie told me she was sure she was pregnant. The only thing that seemed upsetting about this was how our families were going to take it, especially her father. He was going to be the biggest obstacle. Mothers have a way of knowing these things.

When she informed her mother, it seemed as if she already knew. We planned this big meeting at my house to inform our parents. I was very nervous about how her father was going to react. I had been going with Nellie for a year and a half but still I had never met her father.

Somehow, we got through it, and it went smoother than I expected. We planned to have a proper wedding and set the wedding day for September. Every payday I would take my whole paycheck and give it to my mother to keep for me. I used only what I had to for carfare and lunch. I had only three months in which to save money and knew I would need every cent I could save.

By the time it was July, I already had enough money to buy the wedding ring and enough to put down as a deposit on a wedding dress. By the beginning of August, things were really hopping. I don't think I can remember a time when Nellie was happier. Every day there seemed to be something to do. I no longer had time to hang out with the fellows. It had been at least a month since I had been to Union Avenue.

Just about that time, we experienced a big crisis: My uncle Willie got arrested. The arrest alone didn't create the crisis. In fact, the day he was arrested, I don't think we even knew. It was what happened a day or two after his arrest that started the big calamity. As he was waiting in the court to be arraigned, he made a desperate attempt to escape. He jumped out the courtroom window, which was about twenty feet to the street. Having injured his leg from the fall, he got up and limped away as best he could. Before he could get very far, he was shot five times. Several policemen and detectives had run to the window, pulled out their guns, and started shooting. Not only did they shoot him, but they also shot some bystanders who were in the area. He had managed to make it around the corner and tried to hide under a parked car. They must have been surprised to find him still alive.

The next day all the newspapers were filled with the story and pictures of some of the injured people.

Willie was about six years older than I was. He was more like an older brother, and I looked up to him. When he went away to the army, I bragged to my friends about him being a soldier. Soon after he was discharged, he started to use drugs. It wasn't too long after, that he started to get arrested. At the time, he was living down on 138th street, the extreme South Bronx. I hadn't seen him much in the last two years, but I often thought about him. Now I was sure it was going to be a few more years before I would see him again. Little did I realize that I would be seeing him a lot sooner than I expected.

About a month before the wedding day, I went downstairs from my house and saw one of the guys from the Dragons walking by. Hawk stopped to talk to me and began filling me in on some of the things that were happening. He told me that the Dragons were fighting with a gang called the Rockets who were about the toughest gang in the Bronx at the time. They were known for killing quite a few people from different gangs.

He went on to say that the reason he was walking by my house was because no one could hang around Union Avenue anymore. The Rockets had started checking the area, looking for members of the Dragons. They had even beaten up some of the Lancers who were not even members of the Dragons. Some of the guys were now hanging around Kelly Street and Intervale Avenue, but it wasn't even safe around there. The Rockets had already gone around there and caught some of the Dragons and beat them up. He also told me to be very careful because the Rockets knew that I had been a member of the Dragons.

I realized later that I should have left well enough alone and not gotten involved, but I felt that I could not abandon the guys. Instead, I went with him to Kelly Street. When we got there, we were amazed to see that practically no one was on the street. We stood and waited for about five or ten minutes before we saw anyone come out of their houses. It was August fifteenth, and it was hot. I knew it must be bad if people were staying inside on days like these.

One of the kids on the block came over to us and told us that about a half dozen of the Rockets had been around about an hour ago and shot at some people they thought were members of the Dragons. It all happened very quickly, and by the time the police came around they were long gone. We continued to wait, and as we did, Hawk filled me in on recent events. Soon other members of the Dragons began showing up and we talked things over with them. Since we were more or less a club that liked to play stickball and go to dances, we were not sure how we were going to resolve this problem.

Indio was a new member to the club; he had been hanging out with us for only a few months. He had come out of prison and had started hanging out with us because he liked one of the girls in the club. He seemed to be the member with the most experience.

"What should we do?" someone asked him.

"There's only one thing we can do. We have to burn 'em back." Burn was the slang word used when one gang went into the street of another gang and openly shot at them. "I'll go if two of you guys will go with me."

In the past I had made claims of how bad I was, and since I was war counselor to the Lancers, I just could not back out now. I thought to myself that I better go, or all the guys would think I was a punk. I should have kept my mouth shut. Here I was, involved in a gang fight when I should have been thinking of Nellie being pregnant.

"How stupid of me to even be here." I thought.

"I'll go," I said.

Before my voice faded, Lefty also volunteered to go. It was all set.

It would be the three of us.

Around 8:30 p.m., we gathered around. We had located the pieces and were soon on our way to Jackson Avenue and 156th Street. One of the girls volunteered to carry the rifle. It was in a flower box, and no one would be suspicious about what was inside. When we were two blocks away she gave the box to Indio and said she couldn't go any further.

Then she quickly disappeared into the crowded street. We continued on.

As we reached 156th street and turned the corner, we could see a large crowd of people in front of the candy store. We crossed over to the other side of the street so they would not see us. I remember thinking how scared all the Dragons were around Kelly Street, and how the Rockets seemed not to have a care in the world. There they were, the music blaring from the jukebox. I guess the last thing they were thinking was that someone would have the nerve to do what we were going to do.

I could actually hear my heart banging in my chest. It was like a stage play with all the lights, and the actors about to perform. We just stood there, no one moving a hair. We didn't even say a word to each other. Each of us waited for the other to move first. Finally, as if moving in slow motion, Indio opened the flower box and pulled out the rifle.

As he pointed the rifle in their direction, he yelled, "Burn!"

Lefty and I followed when the first shot rang out. We were all firing in the direction of the crowd. People were falling to the ground. The bullets hit some; others threw themselves down trying to avoid getting shot. We all emptied our guns at about the same time, and then we started running in the opposite direction from where we came. We kept running until we felt safe enough. We ran at the top speed for about five or six blocks and finally had to slow down.

After resting for a moment, we decided to split up. Indio stuffed the rifle in his pants and went limping off in one direction; Lefty disappeared in another direction. I went in the direction of my house and did not stop until I got home.

Everyone was in bed by the time I arrived, so I went to my room and jumped in bed. I didn't want to think about anything that had happened. Blacking it all from my mind, I went to sleep.

IV

THE NEXT MORNING MY MOTHER OPENED the door to the room and called me. It would always take two calls before I got up to start getting dressed for work. On this morning, it only took one call. I was hoping that by the time I was dressed, I would realize that what happened last night was a dream. But it was no dream; it was real. I wondered how many of those we shot were dead. What would my family think if they knew what had happened? What would Nellie think? How could I have done such a terrible thing?

I could not think about it from that point of view, so I started to blame them. Why did they have to come around, messing with us? Blaming them for what we had done made me feel better for the moment. I went into the bathroom and was brushing my teeth when I heard a loud knock at the door.

I knew it had to be the police. My first instinct was to run, but I had nowhere to go.

My mother knocked on the bathroom door and told me to come out. When I opened the door, I was shocked at the number of police who were in the house--even outside in the hallway.

My mother was hysterical by now and asking what had happened. One of the detectives told her I had shot a lot of people last night. I was placed in a pair of handcuffs and taken out of the apartments. As I was being taken out of the hallway, I saw even more policemen coming down from the roof of the building.

This is it. I told myself. It's all over. I'll probably never see the streets again.

As I was led out of the building, I saw all the police cars lining both sides of the street. I couldn't help but think, "Why do they need so many police to arrest me?"

I looked in the police cars and saw that they had also arrested some of the Rockets. I was surprised and couldn't figure out what had happened.

When we arrived at the police station, I saw Lefty being taken out of another police car. I tried looking around quickly to see if Indio had also been arrested. Before I had a chance to look at all the cars, I was rushed into the police station and taken directly up the stairs to one of the interrogation rooms.

Five minutes later, the door opened, and Lefty was brought into the room. I was glad to see him. Now I had someone to talk to. Maybe Lefty knew more about what had been happening, why so many of the Rockets had been arrested along with us.

We had been in the room about ten minutes when the door opened once again, and in came Indio. In a way I was relieved to see that the three of us had gotten arrested. It avoided anyone having to get beat up to tell on each other. As the three of us talked we still could not figure out why so many of the Rockets had been arrested. As far as we knew, we were the ones who had done the burning.

Once again, the door opened, and this time four detectives entered the room. One of them shouted over to us.

"So, you guys are the Dragons. Let's see how bad you guys really are. If I don't get some real answers, I'm going to bust me a few heads. I knew you were the guys who did the burning on the Rockets last night, and I want to hear the whole story. You guys don't know how lucky you were that you didn't kill someone last night."

It was the answer to the question that none of us dared to ask. I could see by the look on Lefty and Indio's faces that they were feeling the same as I did. We had some hope. My joy was not even affected by the loud voice of the detective as he continued to speak.

"I'm going to leave you guys in this room for a few minutes, and when I come back, you better have your story straight."

Three of the detectives left the room, but one stayed behind. "Give me a moment to speak to them," he said to the others.

As the last one out closed the door behind him, the detective continued. "Look. You guys seem like a nice bunch of kids. I can understand how guys can get caught up in these gang fights. The best thing to do is tell the truth and the judge will probably have some consideration for you."

He went on to tell us how the policemen were aware that the Rockets were a bunch of troublemakers.

"If any of you have to do time, it won't be much. Maybe even probation. But you have to be careful with Lieutenant Smith. He's the one who spoke to you when we came into the room. He can hurt you guys real bad. Now think about what I said. We can get this thing over real fast."

He left the room, and we were alone again. I looked at Indio since he was the one who had the most experience. Indio had been out of jail only a few months. He had done about three years of a five-year sentence in Woodburn. I felt bad for him because he was going to end up in jail again.

This was Lefty's first arrest. He might be the one of the three of us to get off on probation. I could go either way; this was my third time arrested. In my two previous arrests, I had not spent more than one night in jail on each.

I was fourteen years old when my first arrest came about. A girl that I was going with ended up pregnant. I couldn't have gone with her for more than a week, two at the most, during this time. I had sex with her twice. After it happened, I stopped seeing her. A few months went by and I had completely forgotten the whole matter until I was arrested and charged with statutory rape. It seemed like such a terrible word for and act that two people agreed to do.

The second time I was arrested was for burglary. I was sixteen and placed on probation for two to three years-- I don't remember exactly. This was the third time, and I knew it was not going to be so simple.

We spent the whole day in the police station, witnesses coming in to identify us, statements being taken. The questions seemed endless.

At about four or five o'clock we were taken down to the lockup in the police station. At the bottom of the stairs some photographers started snapping pictures with their cameras. We were placed in separate cells and told we had to stay there until we went to court the next day.

The cell consisted of a wooden bench and a toilet bowl. There was no mattress, pillow, or anything to cover myself with. I knew that Lefty was in the cell next to me because he was the first to be locked up. I was next. Indio was last, so I didn't know where they put him. We were not able to see each other but we were able to talk. It took us a while to get used to the deep echo that bounced off the steel and cement walls. After about an hour, though, we were singing and telling each other jokes.

We knew we would have to go to court the next day. In order to not think about it, we killed most of the night by tapping a conga beat on the steel wall: ana bacoa, coa, coa, ana bacoa, coa, coa. Our only break was when we stopped to pool our money together to buy something t to eat. A guard was good enough to go out and buy us some sandwiches and coffee at inflated prices. He must have had a lot of overhead.

After our music therapy was over and we felt it was time to get some shut-eye, I laid down on the wooden bench and tried to imagine it was a soft mattress. I was now confronted with what I had done. I thought of Nellie. I wondered how she was taking all of this.

"By now she surely must know" I said to myself. She must be angry with me, after all we had planned and all the things we had bought for the wedding. If only I could get out of this. If only I hadn't run into Hawk in front of my house.

I tossed and turned for a while before I fell asleep.

In the morning I was awakened by the sound of the guards keys being rattled on the bars in front of my cell. For a moment, I almost rolled over, turning my back to the door to wait for my mother to call me again. But as I felt the hard wood under me, the reality of where I was suddenly hit me. I moved to a sitting position on the edge of the bench. I had my elbows on my knees and my hands holding up my head when the officer opened my cell and gave me some coffee and a Danish. I wasn't accustomed to eating anything before washing up, but I didn't dare complain about the room service.

After breakfast, they took us to the bathroom where we were supposed to wash up. The bars of soap and sink were still dirty from when we had used them the day before after being fingerprinted. From behind the cells that we were in, I could see some of the members of the Rockets. Up until then I didn't realize there were more cells in that place. The police had been keeping us apart for fear that we would start fighting in the police station.

I could see about six or seven Rockets. I learned later that the reason they had gotten busted was after we had finished burning them that night, they got a large group of their gang together and went to Kelly Street to retaliate. When they reached Kelly Street, they saw some of the Dragons and started shooting at them. One of the Dragons started shooting back and shot one of them in the leg. The cops came quickly and were able to catch some members from both gangs. From the bunch arrested, they were able to get the information that led to our arrests.

All I could do in the bathroom was wash my hands and face and rinse out my mouth. I thought about not having a toothbrush or toothpaste or even a comb. I didn't worry about it too long, though. I had other problems. Besides, I was sure that no one who got arrested came prepared with an overnight bag.

As hard as I have tried, I cannot remember going to court that day. All I know is that I was given a fifteen-thousand-dollar bond. Indio was given a high bond, and Lefty only five thousand.

When we arrived at the Bronx County Jail late that day, all the other prisoners were in their cells sleeping. Indio and I were assigned to the same tier. Lefty was sent to another tier. As we were waiting to go up to our tier, the guard opened a large panel. The door on the panel was about four feet high by four feet wide. Inside the panel were two rows of switches. He pulled one, and we entered into a small area. He slammed one gate behind us before he opened the next one. We entered the tier, and the last gate closed behind us.

As we walked down the tier with our bedding in our arms, the guard told me that I had cell forty-seven. We reached Indio's cell first. The guard pulled another switch, and the gate to his cell opened. I continued walking until I reached forty-seven, about five cells down from Indio's cell closed, and then mine opened up. I entered, and as the gate closed behind me, I wondered how long I was going to be there.

The next morning, we were awakened and instructed to clean our cells before breakfast. Some of the prisoners were let out of their cells to clean up the tier. As they swept and mopped, they would look into my cell, but they didn't say anything to me. Indio had warned me about what this place was going to be like.

"It's important to act cool," he said, "but be ready for anything. And be very careful how you talk to people. Don't ever let anyone try to get over on you. Once any of the inmates feel they can get over on you, you'll lose respect. If that happens, then they'll try to turn you into a girl. It's better to fight, no matter if you get beat up and sent to the hole. Eventually they'll stop messing with you." Then he told me, "It's really not too bad in the county jails. Being sent to prison is a lot worse."

I knew I had to start getting my mental attitude ready in the event I ended up having to go to prison. I thought about Willie. He was in this same jail somewhere, but I didn't know what floor he was on. I wondered if he knew I was here. Lefty had told me that a person could be in the Bronx County Jail for months and not see someone unless you happened to go to court on the same day. I decided I couldn't count much on Willie's reputation to help me. Then I realized that Indio and I were on the floor with the prisoners who were under twenty-years of age. Willie was in the adult section, so that made my chances even slimmer.

I was thinking that if he did see me, he would probably give me a kick in the ass for doing what I did.

The men who were cleaning the floor were finished, and the guard began walking up the tier, checking it out. He seemed to be satisfied and pulled the switch that opened all the cells at the same time.

He yelled down the tier, "Everybody out of your cells."

I stepped out and the cell gate closed behind me. As I glanced up and down the tier, I could not see anyone I knew. I then started walking toward Indio. As he began moving in my direction, one of the prisoners took a swing at him. The punch landed somewhere near his temple and caught him completely by surprise. I instantly rushed toward the guy who had hit him. The guy was aware of me and braced to defend himself. As I lunged at him, another prisoner stopped me short.

"Let them go at it fair!" he yelled.

Indio had enough time to recuperate. From his crouching position, he hit the guy full force. From the way the guy's face shifted, I assumed he had broken his jaw.

The guard came running and started yelling, "Hey, you guys, break it up!"

When things cooled down, he ran back to the front and called for help. Within minutes, the famous jack-up squad appeared on the floor. All the prisoners were told to lock in. When the two gates leading to the tier were opened, all you could hear were the voices of the guards as they looked for the guys who were involved in the fight.

The guard who was assigned to the floor was walking outside the gate, looking from cell to cell to point them out. When he passed in front of my cell, I held my breath, just waiting to hear him say "call forty-seven", but he just kept walking. He returned to the front, and then I heard the cells open. The four huge guards must have had a picnic on Indio! It lasted only about five minutes, but it seemed much longer to me. I'll bet it seemed even longer to Indio.

I heard the cell door close, and the guards walked down to the other cell. I heard the sound of another door opening. The guy in that cell started to tell the guards that he thought his jaw was broken. I guess they figured he had had enough, or maybe they didn't want to hit him for fear they would have to take the blame for the broken jaw. At any rate, within a few minutes he was removed to the hospital, and Indio was removed and put in another cellblock. I was lucky the guard didn't see me try to get into the fight.

The guard on duty came back and stopped in front of my cell. "Laguna, you got any enemies on the floor?" he asked.

"None that I know of."

"Well, you're going to stay locked in until I'm sure."

He then went back and opened all the cells except mine.

Breakfast had come up, and all the prisoners were lined up getting their food. I saw them as they went past in front of my cell. Suddenly my door opened without me expecting it to. I stuck my head out the door and saw the tier boy coming with a tray in his hands. I moved back in the cell as he handed it to me. The door closed, and I sat on the edge of my bed to eat.

My first day in jail was already a disaster. I was having mixed feelings about survival. I was alone now. From here on I had to do it on my own. I was always bad, but before I always had people behind me. I didn't have anyone now. I remembered Indio's words to me: "It's better to fight, even if you get your ass kicked. People in prison can respect that. When they know that you won't back down, they won't mess with you. That's the first rule of survival."

The next day I was allowed out of my cell with the rest of the prisoners. I was glad to get out of that confining space. Small tables made of aluminum were attached to the bars, so after breakfast I sat down at one of the tables and began talking to another prisoner. He had been there for about thirty days. I asked him about the guy who had the fight with Indio. He explained to me that one of the gang members who had gotten shot was his cousin.

"When he read in the paper about the shooting," he explained, "he made a big statement about how he hoped the guy who shot him would come on this tier. Then when you guys showed up, he had to back up his statement."

While we were talking, a few other prisoners joined in on our conversation. They all had read the story in the newspaper and wanted to hear more of what had happened. I explained as much as I knew, and even added a few more details to make it more exciting. Most of the younger prisoners were very impressed by the whole thing, but some of the other prisoners, mostly the older guys, didn't seem interested.

In the afternoon when they called for the guys who had visits, my name was among them. I had a visitor, and I was hoping that it was Nellie. Then I learned that prisoners were only allowed visits from their immediate families. Since Nellie was my girlfriend, she was not allowed to visit me.

When I got to the visiting room, I was surprised to see that it was Nellie. She had used my sister's birth certificate to get in. When I went to the booth, I could see she had tears in her eyes. The visiting room did not offer much privacy. It had a long row of little cubicles with a thick glass that allowed you to see your visitor only from the waist up. If the person stood back, you could see their entire body, but so would the people in the booth next to you. It had a telephone hookup so that you could talk. I was always suspicious of those phones and often wondered if someone was able listen in. Everything was closed off so that any physical contact was impossible.

It was very difficult trying to talk. What could I say that wouldn't be painful? I could not justify anything I had done. I had cheated her out of the wedding, and the worst part was that none of this had to happen. I had no excuse to give to her. If I had been arrested for stealing or for drugs or anything else, at least I would have had a reason for being here, but this was so senseless.

The first five or ten minutes of our visit were spent on small talk, almost as though I were not in jail at all. But soon the small talk came to an end.

She looked at me straight in the eyes, and as her eyes became filled with tears, she asked, "Why?" Why did you do such a crazy thing, Miguel?"

I had no answer to give her.

"I don't know how I can face this all by myself," she sobbed, reaching for a tissue to dry her eyes.

I could not offer her anything. I could not even say a word. I just sat there as she cried. If only I could have just put my arms around her and held her close to me! But that was impossible.

The visiting time was over, and I had to leave. The guard was waiting for me to hang up the phone, so I had to leave her. She just stood there, crying as I walked away.

I have no way of putting into words the pain that I felt that day. In the past I could always do something about any situation. This time I was completely helpless. I could do nothing but walk away and leave her there, alone and crying.

I spent the next five months in that same cell and I don't remember having any problems with anyone. Nellie never missed a day visiting me. I could see her from the window that was across from my cell. She would come with Ara, Willie's wife, at the time. She would come to see Willie every day. They were both pregnant at the time, but nevertheless, they were both there every day.

I could not get out on bond because I was on probation when I was arrested. That meant that if my family came up with ten percent, which was fifteen hundred dollars, I would still be there for the violation of probation.

Having to be in the county jail for five months was very hard. It was not a place that was designed for people to do long amounts of time. Its purpose was just to hold people while they awaited the disposition of the court. Since there was nothing to do, you had to find things to keep yourself from going crazy. Talking with other prisoners and playing cards was all there was to do when you were out of your cell. I would also buy the newspapers every day and save them to read in my cell at lock-in time.

About half the people in my cellblock were there for drugs or drug-related arrests. Most of the conversations that took place were centered on drugs. Since this seemed to be the "in" thing. I found myself talking about my one experience with drugs. However, the one time I had used, two years ago, did not qualify me as a drug addict. I had to fabricate tales so I could impress them. Being in jail for gang fighting was not such a hip thing. After all there was no high or money involved in gang fighting.

This kind of exposure was having its effect on me. Without realizing it, I was developing a curiosity about drugs. According to my reasoning, if so, many people were using drugs, it must really make y you feel good.

The summer ended and so did the fall. As the months went by, Nellie grew closer and closer to having the baby. Finally, on January 6, 1953, she gave birth to our son. We named him Miguel Laguna III. It was about one or two weeks before I was to go up for sentencing. Even though I was in jail, I remember how proud I was when I became a father. I even bought cigars and handed them out to all the prisoners in my cellblock. If only I could have been on the outside, I think I would have been the happiest man in the world.

V

THE DAY FOR SENTENCING FINALLY CAME. As Indio and I sat in the bullpen waiting for the judge to call us, we talked about our chances. Indio kept telling me that I had the best chance between us. He didn't give himself much hope. He had already done time and violated his parole. He was certain he was going to get some heavy time. I was trying to have the same outlook, but deep down inside I wanted to go free. I didn't want to go to prison. I was hoping the judge would be lenient with me; after all, I had already spent about five months in jail, and besides that, I was now a father. Surely, he could not be so cold-blooded that he would send me to prison.

I thought to myself, "if the judge was to give me a break, I could walk out of the court with my family. I could go home and not have to return to that cell."

I prayed that God would touch his heart. I would promise anything if only I could go free.

When we heard our names, we got up and stood by the gate. The gate was opened, and we were led down the corridor towards the courtroom.

I kept murmuring to myself, "Please, God. Please, God."

The door to the courtroom was opened, and we were led over to the judge. Lefty joined us as we stood there in front of this man who had so much power. Lefty had been out on bail since the second day of our arrest.

I looked around in the courtroom and saw Nellie with my family. She had the baby in her arms. It was the first time I had seen him. He looked so small as she turned him in my direction so I could have a better look.

The voice of the judge drew my attention. He was addressing both the defending and prosecuting attorneys.

"Do either of you have anything to say before I pronounce sentence?" he asked them.

I stood there as the lawyers clumsily went through their plea for the court to have mercy on us. The judge gave me the impression that he could not care less what the lawyers were saying. I tried to look as humble as I possibly could. All the toughness was gone from me. I don't think anyone noticed my knees shaking.

The judge then asked if they had finished.

"We have, Your Honor," was the reply.

"Society must be protected from such acts of violence," he said, all the while searching for some papers on his desk. "You boys have committed a senseless brutal crime."

He then picked up what he was looking for and addressed Lefty.

"I hereby sentence you to five years at Elmira Reception Center. Sentence suspended with five years' probation."

That meant he wouldn't have to do any time. Lefty looked relieved.

"Miguel Laguna, I sentence you to an indefinite period, not to exceed more than five years, at Elmira Reception Center." He then looked at Indio and said, "I sentence you to no less than two- and one-half years or no more than five years at Elmira Reception Center."

I was sort of surprised that I didn't feel as much emotion as I thought I would. Lefty said he was sorry as we shook his hand. Indio and I were then escorted back to the bullpen. I didn't have much of a chance to look back to see Nellie and the baby because the guards where blocking our view as we left the courtroom.

We sat and talked about how glad we were that the whole thing was over. Indio was telling me that the five months we spent at the Bronx county jail would be cut off the back part of the five years, which made it four years and seven months.

"That's good," I said, but I really didn't care. Five months off the back of my sentence wasn't going to change much.

One of the guards came to the bullpen. "Which one of you is Laguna?" he asked.

"Here," I said.

"You have a visitor."

I was surprised. I had never gotten a visit while I was in court.

The guard led me to a room and opened the door. I entered a room similar to the visiting room at the jail. When I got to the booth, no one was on the other side. I waited about five minutes. Then I saw my Aunt Ramona with the baby. He must have been two weeks old and didn't move much. His hair was jet black and his eyes rolled around, not really looking at anything. He was the best-looking baby I had ever seen. I wanted to hold him in my arms but the wall between us made it impossible.

I suddenly realized that I had totally ignored my Aunt Ramona. She was one of those rare people who were truly genuine. It was her husband who got me the job and taught me the tool and die trade. She was my father's sister, and I could remember how excited my sisters and I used to get when we went to visit them on Sundays. Although I think she favored my older sister, she always treated all of us well.

After a few minutes of small talk, the visit was over. I was led back to the bullpen to await transportation back to the jail. After so many months of being brought to court, I was glad this was my last.

As I entered my cellblock most of the guys were waiting for me to tell them how much time I got. I told them I got five years in a boasting sort of way. I put on a front and acted as if going to Elmira was no big thing.

It was a different thing when lock-up came. I was alone in my cell, and I was thinking about those five years. I think that being alone made me finally realize the reality of what those five years really meant. I knew I would have to do at least two years, and that was if I didn't get into any trouble. Two years of being away from Nellie and my family. The others all had ten to twenty, fifteen to thirty, twenty to forty, and the one with the most time had thirty to sixty. Looking at it that way, I thought I had it made. Five years was like a weekend in the Catskills compared to them.

We were all put into patty wagons and taken across to New Jersey. There were about thirty-five of us altogether. We were put on a train that would take us directly to Elmira, New York.

The trip took about seven or eight hours. When we arrived in the town of Elmira, we were driven by car to the reception center. It was snowing, and as we got close, I could see the wall and the gun towers. I didn't know how old the place was but I had heard that they kept Civil War prisoners there. It was easy to believe.

We were taken inside the prison, and the shackles and handcuffs were removed. It felt good to be able to move around free after being confined for so many hours. We were then examined for any contagious disease. We were even checked for gonorrhea. We were stripped of all our clothing and then marched to the shower. I was surprised to see that one of the guys from Brooklyn had a wooden leg. The guy had to hop around on one leg while the guard checked his false leg. It was strange seeing a naked guy without a leg.

Before entering the shower, they gave us two pairs of dungarees and two shirts, a towel, wash cloth, two sets of underwear, shoes, socks, a navy-type pee coat, belt (the kind that had a military buckle), sheets, pillowcase, blanket, soap, toothpaste, and toothbrush. Then we were allowed to shower.

After showering we were taken to our cells. When we reached the cellblock, I looked up and couldn't believe my eyes. The cellblock was incredibly long. It had three tiers and bridges crossing from one side to the other. I believe it was bigger than a football field. I had never seen anything like it before. (I've also never seen anything like it since. Even the cellblocks on Rikers Island were not as big.)

We were then taken to a row of cells that were all empty. One by one we entered them, and the doors were close When I entered my cell, I gave it a quick glance and then proceeded to make up my bed. I was really tired from that long trip, so the only thing I wanted to do was go to sleep. I lay in the bed, and within five minutes I was dead to the world.

I awakened the next morning to the sound of a loud bell. After washing up and waiting for our turn to come for breakfast, I picked up the magazine in my cell that I hadn't taken time to look at the night before. I just flipped through the pages and glanced at the pictures. Soon my door opened, and I stepped out and stood in front of the cell. We were then marched to the mess hall.

We ate in the mess hall as the general population. I saw a lot of people I knew from the street and from the Bronx County Jail. Just as I was going to wave hello, Indio stopped me and said we were not allowed to say anything to the general population.

"Just look and give a quick nod, and they'll nod back," he instructed.

So that's how I did it, and it worked.

It was a long walk to and from the mess hall, a trip we had to make three times a day. But I did not mind at all. It helped break up the day.

The first two weeks were very hectic. We had to take a lot of tests. Elmira Reception was a place that tested and screened all prisoners. From there they were sent to other reformatories that would best suit them. The men with mental problems would be sent to Matawan. If you had lower than average intelligence, you would go to Woodburn. Average prisoners went to Coxsackie. Anyone who was higher than average went to Wall Kill. Some who were older would stay in Elmira Reformatory, which was just next-door. Within the first two months, it would be decided where we were going to be sent.

We didn't have much to do, so we spent a lot of time in our cells. Most of the recreation time was spent learning how to march. We never saw the gym. The only time we left our cells was to go to the dining room and to the library once a week. Other than that we were taken to shower once each week, it was really hard on me being in my cell all those hours. I tried to do as much as I could so I wouldn't go crazy.

In my cell was a broom with the handle cut down to about six inches. I rolled up a pair of socks into a ball. With the broom as my paddle, I played my own style of paddleball. It helped me in two ways: the most important was that it helped the time pass; the other was the exercise it provided for me.

At night it was a lot better because we would listen to the radio: Sam Spade, the Lone Ranger, Jack Benny, and my favorite, Amos, and Andy.

One morning as we were let out of our cells for breakfast, we learned that one of the guys who had come from New York with us had hung himself in his cell. He came from a well-to-do family. His father was a big executive with Eastman Kodak. He was sent here because he constantly got arrested for stealing cars. I used to get along good with him. He loved cars and would always talk about models that I had never even heard of. He would steal cars just to go joy riding. His father had gotten fed up with him and thought that jail would cure him from stealing. He was given an indefinite sentence of up to three years. He wasn't what I considered a real criminal.

Actually, I didn't think he belonged there at all. I was really surprised that he would do something like that.

That morning when we were all standing in front of our cells as we always did, he didn't come out. The guard waited a few minutes and then came walking down the tier to see why. When he reached his cell, he just stood there. Without saying a word, he slid the door shut.

The guard walked back to the front and yelled "Front face." When we were all facing front, he yelled, "Close it up."

I knew they couldn't have taken him anywhere because the guard would have known. I wanted to look in his cell as I passed in front of it. The cells there had no bars; instead, the doors had a small opening so the guards could look in. Since I was short, I had to walk on my toes to see inside the cell. I had to look fast without stopping. As I passed, I saw his body hanging underneath a ventilator. He had tied a piece of his sheet through a hole in the ventilator, and from there, around his neck. I could not see his face because it was turned the other way, but I knew he was dead. I wondered how long he had been hanging there.

As we were walking to the mess hall, I felt sick. I was lightheaded and tried to think of something else so that I wouldn't faint. When I finally sat down, I turned to Indio and told him what I had seen. I wasn't aware that he had also looked in the cell and had seen the guy hanging there. Indio told me not to say anything and to act as if I had not seen a thing.

"Since you're being shipped to Coxacki, it's better that you don't say anything to anyone. They might send you to Mata Juan with all those crazy guys."

That was all he had to say. Maybe he was exaggerating, but I wasn't going to take that chance.

When we got back to our cells, the guy was gone.

Later that day, one of the other inmates asked a guard what had happened to the guy. The guard told him the guy had gotten sick and had to be sent to a hospital outside the jail. Maybe I was a little naïve, but I think they were trying to cover up for our own good. After all, the guy hung himself. Certainly, he was not the first, and he wouldn't be the last. But the fact was, I knew what went down, and it bothered me a lot. But I had to survive, so I kept it all inside.

VI

WAS ON MY WAY TO COXACKI, and even though I wasn't sure how long I would be there, I knew this would be the place that I would go home from. It was another very long, agonizing ride. Coxacki was much closer to New York City. In the three months I spent in Elmira, I never got a visit. I had written and received mail from Nellie and my mother, but it was much too far away from New York City for them to visit me. Now, at least, they would be able to visit.

As we got closer, the driver pointed the jail out to us. It didn't look like a jail. It was very different from Elmira. It could have been a military school. We repeated almost the same procedure we had undergone that first day at Elmira. Then we were put in quarantine for two weeks. In those two weeks we were told the rules and regulations, we were given physicals again, and were given inoculations. They didn't tell me what they were for, and I didn't ask.

From the quarantine block, we could look out into the yard. I had heard that it was segregated, not only by race, but also by the city or town the prisoners were from. Only the Spanish corner had no limitations of city or town. I could see the Spanish corner from the window. They all stood together in one area as did other groups in other parts of the yard. These corners had windows that had to be respected; no one was permitted to enter unless they asked permission. Every corner had an owner, and only he could decide who could be in it. If you didn't know him, you had to know someone who could speak for you before you could enter. If you were not allowed in any corner, then you would have to stay in the creep corner.

The creep corner was not really a corner; it was out toward the center of the yard. It had no windows and no wall to it, a kind of no-man's-land.

In the center of the yard was the track, although it wasn't laid out like an official track. It was called the track because the inmates would walk around the yard on it, forming a large circle.

From the window I could see the whole layout. I could see a few people in the Spanish corner whom I knew from the street and from jail. Although I was a bit worried about not getting into the Spanish corner, I kept trying to convince myself that I shouldn't have any problems.

I finally hit population and was accepted into the Spanish corner very easily.

In this institution, everyone had to either work or go to school. I started to go to school, attending machine shop in the morning and drafting in the afternoon. Since I had taken trumpet lessons when I was younger, and had even played in an amateur band, I now joined the band for something to do in my spare time. I also knew how to play congas, a percussion instrument played with the hands and used in Latin bands.

Things were going along very smoothly for me. I made some friends and that helped fill my time. We would always look out for each other. The first few months went by very quickly. The machine shop began to bore me. I was doing projects that I had already done in high school. I made a request to work outside in the labor gang, and they agreed to this. The work was hard, but I didn't mind.

During the winter the big sport was boxing. I always wanted to get into it, but up to that point in my life I never had the opportunity. I got involved and had seven fights. Even though I won the first four fights, I really wasn't too crazy about it. I got into some tougher competition and lost the next three fights. Being knocked out cold in my seventh fight made me hang up the gloves. I figured boxing wasn't my best talent.

I got along pretty good with most of the guys in the Spanish corner, but there was one guy I didn't like at all. He was doing five years, just like me, but he had already done over four of the five. He had never made parole because he kept getting into all sorts of trouble. Most of the inmates would try not to get involved with him. He was always up to no good. What I mostly disliked about him was that he was always trying to abuse the younger inmates, especially when they were small and good-looking. If he was talking with someone and a young boy passed by, he would always make a comment like, "Man, look at that young sweet thing. Ain't he fine?"

I had seen and heard that kind of talk from a lot of the inmates, but with most of them it was just talk. This guy meant every word of what he was saying. I often wondered what kind of person he was on the outside. Being eighteen and good-looking at the time didn't make it any easier for me. I had gained the respect of most of the men, but I just knew that at some point I was going to have trouble with this guy. I kept remembering Indio's words: "It's better to fight and go into solitary than to have somebody make a girl out of you."

About six months after my arrival, I was called into the deputy warden's office. While I was waiting to go in, I tried to imagine what he wanted to see me about. He was the person you had to see if you got into any kind of trouble. When I entered his office, he showed me a letter Nellie had sent to me. He asked me who she was. I knew what he was getting at. Nellie had been writing me under the presence that she was my sister. Girlfriends were not allowed to write to the inmates. I knew if I lied to him, I would be in trouble because I had also answered her letters pretending the same. I told him that she was my girlfriend and about the baby. He said that didn't matter; she could not write me anymore. This was a blow for me: Nellie was the most important reason for me to try to get out of there fast. I had to keep my mouth shut when he told me to leave.

Up until that time I had not gotten into any trouble. I always made sure of that. As I entered the yard, I didn't feel like talking with anyone. One of my buddies, a guy by the name of Munge, came over and asked what was wrong. I told him about the incident. He told me that I should be cool and not to let this get me upset. We kept talking for a while, and soon I started to feel better. Some other fellows came over and we started a jam session in the yard. I was beating on one of the benches and the others were singing. It lasted until it was time to lock up.

I was in a dormitory, and it was a lot better than being in a cellblock. When we went up for the night, we still had time to socialize and play cards. Whiz was the most popular game played. Inmates would play for cartons of cigarettes. I always tried to avoid heavy gambling. We could get only three cartons of cigarettes a month, and since that was enough for me, I didn't want to lose them gambling.

The months continued to go by, and I really missed those letters from Nellie. She always used to send me pictures of the baby. I remember how she would explain what little Mikey was doing when she took his picture. Even though my mother continued to write and send me pictures, it was not the same.

In all the time I had been there, I had never seen Nellie. My family visited me almost every month. That was something to look forward to, but I could not see Nellie and the baby. If only we had been married before all this happened, things could have been so very different.

VII

ONCE AGAIN, THE CHRISTMAS HOLIDAYS WERE here. It was the second Christmas in a row that I would not be with my family. I had a great job now; I was working in the rear gate. Everyone who worked outside had to go through the rear gate. I was in charge of keeping the area clean and helping to load and unload the trucks that made deliveries of all sorts. I also had to go to the different shops and the hospital to collect the garbage and take it to the incinerator to burn.

There was one part of the job that I didn't like. That was that the inmates were always trying to get me to smuggle contraband into the prison. I constantly kept refusing to get involved with any of that.

One day while we were in the yard, one of the guys in my corner invited me to walk the track with him. I went, and at first he didn't get into anything heavy. As the conversation moved along, however, he started telling me that some of the guys at the dairy farm where he worked had gotten together and made some moonshine. They had made it for the holidays and they had it stashed outside. It was too much for them to smuggle in alone.

I said to him, "Why don't you guys just drink it out there?"

"That won't work. There are too many guys in on it and most of them don't work on the farm. We've got to get it into the yard."

I hesitated.

"You could make a lot of cigarettes on the deal," he said, making the whole idea more tempting

"How much are they willing to pay?" I wanted to know.

He looked straight at me and said, "Whatever you charge."

I thought of how much trouble I could get myself into. I knew I could smuggle in the stuff, but there was always that slim chance that I might get caught, and then I would be in serious trouble.

"How much of that stuff do they want to bring in?" I asked.

"About three gallons."

"Are you crazy? How am I going to bring in that much?"

"Calm down. You don't have to bring it in all at once. Christmas is still three days away."

"I need some time to think about it," I told him, trying to calculate the risks. "I'll have the answer for you in the morning."

We left the track and returned to the corner. I talked about this with Munge and a couple of other guys I was tight with. Munge told me I had better think about it carefully. If the booze got in, a lot of guys were going to get drunk and start acting crazy. If the guards were to notice. it would be big trouble.

Orlando, another of my tight friends, told me I should tell them that I wanted about twenty cartons of cigarettes. That way I was not really saying no, but they wouldn't be able to come up with the cigarettes and would just try to find another way. That sounded like a good idea. I still had a little time to talk with the guy again, so I called him out to the track.

"I've got a lot to lose if I get caught," I explained. "It's going to cost you guys twenty cartons of cigarettes."

I almost jumped out of my shoes when he said he was sure they would be willing to come up with the cigarettes. I had to come through now. I just couldn't back down. I had to have the booze in for the big Christmas show since the plan was for them to drink it before the show started.

The show was to take place in the gym. The location was good, I decided, because there they could get stoned and probably go without notice. It wasn't unusual to laugh out loud and be boisterous at the shows. The prison staff expected the inmates to have a good time.

The next morning, I met with the guy who had approached me. He told me he would have about ten cartons after work.

"Okay, you're on. But I can't bring it in if it's in large gallon bottles. We'll have to think of a way to get some smaller bottles or containers."

I spent all that morning thinking of how I was going to get all that booze in. What could I use to break up those three-gallon jugs into smaller portions? The more I thought about it, the more I worried that I was not going to be able to figure out a way to do it. If I got caught, it would mean a long time in segregation, and the parole board would probably deny me. I could lose maybe six months or even a year, depending on the deputy warden. It would also mean my job.

The more I thought about it, the more I regretted becoming involved in something like this, but it was too late; I could be in worse trouble if I didn't do it. These guys were counting on having a good time for the Christmas show, and anyone who messed with these plans was going to be in big trouble.

All that morning at work I kept thinking how I was going to get the booze in. As I made my rounds collecting the trash, I kept my eyes open, trying to find something small enough to use. Then, when I entered the laundry room pushing my garbage cart, I saw the men sorting the clothing that was to be washed. Whites were on one side, and pants and shirts on the other. They always used some cloth gloves when handling soiled laundry. Suddenly it came to me. If I could get some plastic rubber gloves, I could use them to bring in the booze. I could always get some rubber gloves at the medic. The medic was my last stop. If everything was the same as always, I shouldn't have any trouble getting gloves.

Luck was with me, and as expected, I was able to get the gloves. When I finished the run, I took the garbage to the incinerator, and as I was separating the stuff to burn from the rest, I took out the rubber gloves. When I counted how many I had, I found that I had far too many. I put what I needed away and burned the rest in the incinerator.

By late afternoon the three gallons of liquor had been dropped off. I had them hidden behind the incinerator. I had to leave everything there because it was almost time to finish work for the I covered everything up as best I could and returned to the rear gate. When I got there, the other outside crews were getting checked in. Everyone who came in from the outside had to be searched as they entered the prison. As usual, I jumped in front of the line to get checked in fast. The guard who was in charge of the rear gate was my boss, and he always checked me right away.

I entered the yard and was quickly approached by the guys. I went out to the track with them, and we started to talk about the deal. Underneath their coats they had the ten cartons of cigarettes. They had them split up between the three of them. I couldn't carry ten cartons by myself, so I took three, put them under my coat, and took them to my corner. I passed them to Munge and then proceeded to get three more, which I gave to Orlando. I grabbed onto the last four and took them to my dorm. I remember thinking that I was due to go to the parole board in February. If I got caught doing this, I would not make parole. After tomorrow this whole thing would be over. One thing was for sure; I'd never get myself into anything like this again. My time was getting too short.

The next day as I went to work, I was still a little worried about bringing in the liquor. It took me about an hour to pour the three gallons into the rubber gloves. It was hard to do it myself. The problem came when I tried to pour and hold the glove at the same time. I had to stretch the edge of the glove over the mouth of a large can and pour just enough so that I could tie the end without spilling any. After spilling quite a lot at first, I finally mastered the procedure. After I had finished and looked down at the gloves, they looked like a pile of cow's tits all spread out on the floor. As I placed them into a garbage can, I was happy and somewhat surprised that they didn't take up much room. I threw some trash on top to cover the gloves. Now all that was left for me to do was bring it in through the rear gate.

I went to this gate and started talking to my boss.

"This will be my last Christmas in jail," I told him.

He looked up at me, and then gave me some advice on things I should do to stay out of trouble when I get out. We always got along well. It was rare to find a prison guard that you could really talk to. I sensed that his advice was very sincere.

In the months that I worked with him, I grew to like him. He had lost his wife about two years ago, and I could tell that he missed her.

She had been killed in an auto accident while they were vacationing in Niagara Falls. The accident happened when they were driving home. I think he blamed himself for her death. He never mentioned that he had been drinking when it happened, but I had a suspicion that he was. All he ever said about that was that he had stopped drinking, but never told me when or how long ago. I wondered what he would do if he found out what I was about to do. It made me feel bad just thinking about it.

If only all this was over with, I thought.

By now it was time to go in for lunch. When I hit the yard, I went out to the track to make the final plans. I was going to bring the liquor in after lunch, and everything had to be right. I needed to have someone to pick it up when I brought it in. Once I dropped it off, my part would be done and I would be home free, but before I could feel relieved, I had to get it in.

The men had someone on the mop gang who would always mop the corridor that led to the rear gate. This was done twice a day. The outside gangs would always leave it dirty whenever they came through, so, it would have to be mopped after lunch and after dinner. A few of the shops were in that corridor, so they had to wait for me to go through before they mopped it. I had to time myself just right. If I came through too early, they might not be ready yet, and if I came through too late, it meant they would all be standing waiting for me. If that happened, the guards would also be waiting and upset. Too much attention would be focused on me to do what I had to do.

The plan was to put the stuff in the mop buckets. It would be a good place because the gloves were almost transparent and would not be seen once they were on the bottom. The buckets would have to be in the halls so the mops could be cleaned when needed. I told them to tell the guys who would be mopping to try to keep the buckets near the shop doors. It would be less obvious and easier that way. That was the plan and I had only one shot at it. Right then I promised God that if I got through this, I would never do anything like it again.

I returned to work after lunch and was getting ready to do my part. I checked my garbage cart to make sure that nothing was showing. I pushed it out from the incinerator and was headed for the rear gate. I looked in again, just to make sure that nothing was showing. As I was pushing the cart up the ramp that led to the gate, I saw my boss waiting for me. At the top of the ramp, he told me to stop. I started to feel my palms sweating and my stomach turning. As I brought the cart to a halt, he walked over to his little booth, reached for his trashcan, and emptied it into my cart. He then returned the empty trashcan to his booth, and I continued pushing the cart toward the rear gate.

As I waited for my boss to open the gate, I tried to look through the small window to see what was happening in the corridor. Before I had a chance to see, my boss was turning the key to slide open the door. I pushed my cart through, and he pushed the gate shut behind me.

I looked down the corridor and everything looked good. The mop buckets were in the right places. As I approached the first shop, I could see only two guards at the far end of the corridor. They were standing together, having a conversation while the crew was mopping toward my end. I knocked on the door so the shop boss could let me in. The door opened, and I went in to get the trash. As I was emptying the trash, one of the inmates began walking toward me, pushing the mop bucket in front of him. I wasn't expecting to do this at the first shop. I thought I would have some time to see if the guards were going to stay at the other end. I emptied the trash and returned it to the shop.

As the shop boss locked the door, the guy who was mopping left the bucket next to me. He had gone down the hall and was mopping his way back toward me. He had placed himself between the guards and me to sort of block their view.

I reached into the garbage cart and took out two of the gloves filled with liquor; that was all I could hold at one time. I placed them into the mop bucket. After looking up and around, I repeated the procedure two more times. The water level in the bucket had risen to the point where I could not put anymore in that bucket. I must have gotten rid of half of the liquor. That was better than I had expected.

I continued down the hall, and at the next shop, the same thing happened but I still wasn't able to unload what I had left. I had only three shops left. I was also getting closer to where the guards were, and the closer I got to them, the harder it would be to make the switch. Finally, I saw the guards coming down the corridor, and I guessed they were on their way to the other end. Most of the mop gang had already worked their way down, and only a couple of guys were left on this end.

As the two guards went past me, I started to get nervous again, not that I was ever completely calm. My nerve meter must have gone from eight to ten. I was just emptying the garbage and as I turned to return the empty trashcan, they were just about reaching me. I was halfway between the shop and the hall when they were going by me. I could almost feel their breath on my neck and feel them grabbing me. It was as though I were frozen there for a long time. Finally, they passed me and I was off, pushing my cart in the opposite direction.

It was going to be more difficult now, having to reach down through all the garbage to get the liquor. I had to stop between the shops so I could move them up closer to the top. Before I reached the next shop, I made the adjustment. The last mop bucket was in place. Once again, the guy mopping had placed himself in position. I made the last drop. By the time I finished all the shops in that area, the whole mop crew was gone.

Everything had gone smoothly, and I felt greatly relieved. It was all over as far as I was concerned. Now the only thing I had to worry about was someone getting caught and ratting on me. The odds were in my favor. Even if someone got caught it was not likely they would tell on me; telling on someone is not something that is done in jail. That's the second thing a person in jail learns.

VIII

THE MEN HAD A GOOD TIME for Christmas, I had my cigarettes, and the whole nightmare was over. The next week was New Years, and I was once again approached to bring in liquor. I told them absolutely and positively no. My time was getting too short for that sort of thing. February was just around the corner, and I wasn't going to let myself get involved with anything again. I'd already done seventeen months in jail, and I wanted to get the hell out of there.

New Year's night was just like any other night. No staying up to bring in the year, no balloons, and no horns. The lights went out at the same time as every other night. It was hard to fall asleep. I was thinking of Nellie, little Mikey, and my family. It felt so unfair that I couldn't be with them. I knew they were all home getting ready to celebrate. It must have been hard for them, too, but at least they were out there together. They were free and I was not. They had each other and I had no one. I felt angry with them because they were going to celebrate without me. Mostly I was angry with myself for being so damn stupid. Why did I do the things I did?

"There's something wrong with me", I told myself. I must be different from other people.

Unless a person has been in prison, it would be hard to know how painful it is. To be deprived of your freedom is something that only a person in jail can feel. Someone is always there to tell you what to do and when to do it. You have nothing to say when you are doing time. You just become someone to a job. No one feels important in jail. It's not the jail itself that makes it hard. Actually, the place is not that bad when you look at it. Your basic needs are met. You can sleep on clean sheets, eat three meals a day, and feel warm in the winter. Maybe that's more than some inmates have when they are free in the streets. It's the confinement that makes it hard.

Most of the inmates don't really care about having their basic needs taken care of. They would rather be homeless bums in the street, as long as it meant they were free. That's how I felt about being in prison.

The month of January went by very slowly for me. I was even more careful not to get into any kind of trouble. Although I was able to stay out of trouble in the eighteen months of time I had done, I was being even extra careful now. I would be going to the parole board in about thirty days. That would mean I could be out in March. I knew I shouldn't be counting on getting out on parole the first time I went before the board. I was there for what was considered a senseless crime, and the parole board was hard on that kind of crime. Instead, I should have been expecting them to deny my first appearance, but there was always a possibility. A slight chance, but a chance.

The night before going to the board was full of fantasies. The miracle was a chance, and a chance was a possibility. I didn't want to think of being denied parole, but still I knew I should prepare myself for a disappointment.

My best friend Munge had been to the parole board the month before and had made parole. He was scheduled to leave in two weeks. In a way I was happy for him, and in another way I wasn't. We had grown very close. Munge, Orlando, and

I. We always hung out together every chance we had. It was always the three of us. Now Munge was leaving, and I was going to miss him.

The next morning, I took extra care to look presentable in front of the parole board. It was the same routine that everyone followed. The yard was full after everyone had finished eating breakfast, and by the time we were ready to go to the board, we were the only ones left. We finally heard the whistle, and the guard said for us to line up. We were marched down the corridor that led to the room where the parole board met.

As we sat on the long bench across the hall from the door, I wondered how long it would take for them to get to me. The guard then switched us around in the order that we would be called. I must have been somewhere in the middle. Each person who went in took about ten to fifteen minutes.

Finally, I was called. I entered and sat down. They asked me a few questions, and I answered them. I was complimented for not having gotten into trouble and told that I would get their decision later. I got up and was escorted out by one of the guards. I had absolutely no indication as to what they were going to do.

After they had finished with all the inmates, we were marched out into the yard. Inmates who had gone before the board were always given the day off. The day before I had told my boss that I wanted to return to work, so he made the arrangement to have me work that afternoon. When I got there, he asked me what I thought. I told him I had no indication. We talked for a while. He was trying to encourage me in the event that I was turned down.

The results were given out with the mail call. We would line up in our form, and after the guard counted us, he would call out the mail. When I was called, I walked to the front and got my envelope from the board. I also got a letter from home. I had to wait for all the mail to be given out before I could leave the line.

When the guard yelled, "Fall out," I immediately opened the envelope. It said that parole was denied at this time, and that I would appear again in May. That was all that was writ on the paper. I was hurt and disappointed. I should have prepared myself for the worst; that way it would not have been so bad. Deep down inside I knew I was setting myself up, but I did it anyway.

Three more months in this place was a joke for some of the other inmates who were doing more time than I was, but to me it meant that I was not going home yet. I had placed the letter I had received from home on the bed, and now I noticed it. I just looked at it for a moment before I reached for it. I removed the staple and took out the letter. (The letters were censored before we got them, which was why it was stapled.) I read the beginning and just couldn't read anymore. After returning the letter in the envelope, I slipped it under my pillow.

I'll wait until later to read it, I told myself.

I lay my head on the pillow and started feeling sorry for myself. Roger, the guy in the bunk next to me, looked over at me and said,

"I guess you didn't make it."

"You're right," was my reply.

"You surely didn't expect parole on the first try, did you?"

I turned to him and said, "I was hoping."

"Well, you shouldn't have got your hopes up."

"I know, I don't want to hear any more about it."

As I thought about what he said, I realized he was right. I had placed myself in that position.

Roger had been in the bunk next to me for about a year. I had met him while we were in Elmira. I was in Coxacki about a month before he arrived. He was an American Indian from Buffalo, New York. He was doing time for stealing cars. He lived in a reservation just outside Buffalo. Up until then I didn't know there were reservations in New York. Although he didn't have much to say, he had a good sense of humor. We got along good from the time we met. He was the kind of person who was slow when it came to making friends.

I didn't realize it at the time, but as I look at it now, I can see that his problem was really alcohol. He started drinking at the age of ten and got into all kinds of trouble because of it. The courts sent him to a juvenile home at the age of thirteen, but he kept running away. He continued like that until finally he ended up in Coxacki with a five-year sentence. He would often talk about drinking and how he would forget what he had done while he was drunk. I could not understand why he (or anyone, as far as that goes) could drink like that. It was beyond me how anyone could drink himself into unconsciousness. It seemed it should be a simple matter to not drink so much. That's how I felt about it. I also felt the same way about drugs. Most of the inmates in the Spanish corner were in prison because of crimes they committed while they were on drugs. To me it seemed it would be simple just to avoid using drugs.

By the time we went down to eat dinner, I was feeling better, and when we returned to the dorm, I started to read my mail. My sister Lydia was going to get married, and the family was all involved with that. I was somewhat disappointed because I was not going to be out in time for the wedding. I had been telling my mother that I thought I was going to make parole, and maybe my sister was expecting me to be there. I decided to write home and give them the bad news. After I had finished writing the letter home, I lay in my bed and started to think. Jail had really done a job on me. I was able to handle the physical part of being here. I had gotten myself involved in as many activities as I could, sports, the band, and my job. I played a lot of whiz, and in between, goofed around a lot, but only with my close friends. That's one thing I had to be careful about. A prisoner couldn't goof around with just anyone. That was one sure way to get in trouble. I had my select group that I could joke around with, but that was the limit. I could not allow anyone else to joke with me either. If that happened, it had to be stopped immediately. I had seen too many crazy things happen because of misunderstandings. In the time that I had spent there, I had seen several inmates get stabbed. Some tried to escape, and some tried to hang themselves in order to get transferred. I saw inmates get beaten so badly by the guards that they had to spend time in the hospital. In spite of all this madness going on around me, I was able to keep my head together. I chose my friends on that basis. Some guys just didn't seem to give a damn what they got into. Those were the guys we had to stay away from.

I had learned the skill to survive. But along with having skill, I also had to have some luck. Jail life was like living in a different world. The whole environment was different. You had to adjust to survive. That's the way it was then, and frankly, I don't think it has changed much today.

I picked up my calendar to see when I would be appearing before the parole board. The board always met around the first week of the month. If I made parole, I would be leaving in June.

It would be four months altogether. That would mean I had completed twenty-two months in all. At that time, we were in the middle of winter, and I had to go through the entire spring. I knew that wasn't very much time, but to me it seemed forever, four more months of dealing with the pressure. I would be nineteen years old in May, and that would mean another birthday in this place. But I didn't have any alternatives. All I could do was wait. After accepting the reality of the situation, I commenced to get on with life in prison.

Munge left on parole. I asked him to go by and see Nellie and the baby. He was to tell Nellie that I should be home in June if I didn't have any more problems. It wasn't long after, that I heard Munge was back on drugs. I was quite disturbed by the news, but I was told it was almost standard procedure. Practically everyone who left on parole who had previously used drugs would return to them. I was particularly disturbed about the news because Munge was a very close friend. We had often talked about what he was going to do when he got out. I knew he really didn't intend to use drugs again.

Looking back, I realize that's what everyone in jail says, but something must happen when they are in the streets. I have never heard anyone who was leaving jail say that the first thing they planned to do when they got out was get high. What happens and what changes is sort of mysterious. I don't know what happens. All I know is that at the time, I was certain I wouldn't have that problem. Or so I thought.

IX

MAY FINALLY CAME, AND ON MAY 1st, I turned nineteen. A week later I went before the parole board for the second time. I went through the same procedure as I had during my first appearance. That evening when I got my slip, it showed the date of my parole as June 21, 1954. I had finally made it.

It took a few days for me to feel the reality that I was going to be free. I was going home. I was going to see Nellie, and I could hold her in my arms. I could see my son and play with him. I would be with my family. When June 21st finally arrived, I got up in the morning and said to myself, "Imagine before this day is over, I'll be with my family. Last night was the last time I'll sleep in this bed."

After breakfast I went to the yard to say good-by to all the guys. Time passed quickly, and before I realized it, I had my state suit on.

With money in my pocket and ticket in hand, I was ready to get on the bus.

As the bus pulled out, I looked back and couldn't believe how nice the place looked. From a long distance, no one would think that such horrible things went on inside those college-like buildings. But I knew. I knew, and I would never forget.

It was an exceptionally beautiful day. The bus ride to New York City would take about two hours. I had waited so long for this day to come, and now I was finally on my way. I wondered if the other passengers knew I had just gotten out of prison. I stood up a moment so I could take off my jacket. I looked around at other people in the bus. No one was paying any particular attention to me. No one seemed concerned about what I was doing. Some were talking to the person next to them; some were just staring out the window; others had their eyes closed as if they were trying to get some sleep. I sat back down and tried to relax.

I stared out the window, not really looking at anything, just thinking of this day so long that I hadn't thought beyond it. I never thought what the second day or third day would be like. I knew I had to think about tomorrow, but I just couldn't. I was in prison this morning, and now I was not.

Finally, I was able to see the New York skyline. The traffic had begun to get very heavy. The bus driver weaved through it very skillfully, and finally we pulled into the bus terminal. I threw my jacket over my arm, picked up my small bag, and joined the line that was leaving the bus. When I stepped off the bus, I met with the other two parolees who had left with me. We all had to report to the parole office. (Funny thing that none of us spoke to each other on the way back. I really didn't know them very well anyway, but I still remember that.)

The three of us walked to catch the subway downtown. About halfway there we decided to chip in and catch a cab. As the cab made its way downtown, we exchanged a few words in idle talk. We just sort of made comments on what we saw through the window of the cab.

When we reached our destination, we went to the office of the Department of Parole, received our instructions, and left. I never saw those two guys again.

Now, at last, I was on the subway headed for the Bronx. I had to change trains on 125th Street. I felt lucky that it wasn't the rush hour yet.

I got off at Prospect Avenue in the Bronx. As I was walking down Longwood Avenue toward Dawson Street where I lived, I couldn't help noticing how small everything looked. It made me feel as if I were walking inside a very large room. I walked down the two blocks to my street, turned the corner, and entered the building. We lived on the top floor. It was four flights up. I took them two steps at a time. I finally reached Apartment 18 and tried to push open the door. When it didn't open, I knocked on the door with my knuckles.

The door opened, and my sister yelled out, "It's him!"

She threw her arms around me, and we hugged each other. Over her shoulder I saw Nellie. She looked so thin and frail. When my sister let me go, I went over to Nellie and took her in my arms and kissed her.

"I'm home at last," I said, almost in tears. "I'm finally home." I looked down then and saw my son Mikey pulling on her leg. I went toward him to pick him up, and he ran behind her, crying at the top of his lungs. I didn't want to shock him any more than he already was, so I backed off. I had plenty of time. We were together now after being apart for so long.

My mother and father arrived later from work, and after all the hugs and kisses, we visited for a while. Later that evening more family and friends came to see me. I stayed home with them all evening. It was great to be home again.

While still in prison, I wrote to the boss where I used to work, and he promised that I could return to my old job. So, the next day, Friday, I went down to the factory. I spoke to the foreman, and he said I could start working on Monday. That was great because I liked that job.

I went back home and spend the rest of the afternoon with Nellie. We talked for hours. Things were hard for me in prison, but she had it hard also. In some ways I felt it must have been just as hard for her. I assured her that things were going to be different now that we were together. That's all that mattered.

We made plans to get married on August 15, 1954, and I began working and saving my money. This time we planned a small wedding in my grandmother's church.

My grandmother had been a member of a Pentecostal Church ever since I could remember. When I was small, my mother would always make sure that my sisters and I would go to church about a month before the Christmas holidays. That way we would be able to get toys before Christmas. The pastor of the church would always be glad when Christmas was over because my cousin Armando and I would drive him crazy.

When the day finally arrived for the wedding, I was sure that as we were going through our marriage vows, the minister must have been thinking about the trouble I had caused him in my youth.

We found a furnished room on Bruckner Boulevard, just a few blocks from my mother's house. Although it was small and we had to share a bathroom with other tenants, somehow, we managed. I worked during the day and Nellie stayed home to take care of Mikey. Everything seemed the way it was supposed to be.

By September Nellie was pregnant again; we were now expecting our second child. By the time the baby began to show, Mikey was two years old. We had to get a bigger place. Apartments were very hard to come by during those years. The only way one could get an apartment was to buy one from someone. When you bought an apartment, you didn't really own it; you just bought the right to live there. I started to save money for that purpose. We didn't have much money left over, so it was hard.

The months passed, and I didn't seem to be making much progress. Things were not looking good with my job, either. The company had been sold and was planning to move out of state.

I reached my twentieth birthday, and Robert was born four days later. Even though we had not gotten an apartment yet and the four of us were still living in one room, we were happy. At that time, I was getting away from getting high on Saturdays. I was getting high only on rare occasions, and then only if someone offered drugs to me. I didn't go around looking for them.

I was now working for a different company. It was a factory that made frames for glasses down on 12th Street. I hated the job and still was barely able to make ends meet.

One day a friend of Nellie's told us that her mother-in-law was selling an apartment for five hundred dollars. We went to see it, and even though it was run down, we wanted to take it. Since I didn't have enough to get it, I decided to see if my mother would lend me the rest of what I needed. She lent me the money, and we moved into the apartment.

Nellie's father bought us a living room set. Her grandmother bought us a dining set. My family also helped with some things, and I went out and bought a bedroom set. We painted, hung curtains, and finally we were settled in. The rent was forty-two dollars per month, which was cheaper than what we were paying for the room. We now had five rooms, and that was a lot better.

X

WAS NOT VERY HAPPY WORKING IN the eyeglass factory. It was a very boring and monotonous job. It was similar to the belt factory that I worked in a few years back. I knew I couldn't stay working in this place; however, I just could not quit without having a better job, so I kept working there and hoping that something better would turn up.

A few months passed, and Nellie was sick all the time. I would get home from work, and she would be in bed with a temperature. At first, we thought it would pass, but it didn't. She just kept looking worse all the time. I took her to the doctor's office, but he didn't seem to know what was wrong. The doctor sent her to have x-rays, and we found out that she had developed tuberculosis. It was a tremendous shock to us. We were not prepared to handle anything like this. She had to go into a hospital, and Robert wasn't even a year old. I didn't know what I was going to do.

Nellie went to St. Joseph's Hospital in South Bronx. I sent Mikey to live with Nellie's grandmother in lower Manhattan. My sister Lydia offered to take care of Robert. I found it hard staying in the apartment alone, so I stayed with my parents. I didn't want to lose the apartment, so, I kept up the rent.

I went down to my sister's house every day. Robert was coming down with a fever now, so I kept taking him to the hospital and hoping he wasn't sick with tuberculosis. But finally, he was diagnosed with TB. He was sent to a hospital in Staten Island by the name of Seaview. It was just for people who had TB, and it was a very long trip getting there. First, I had to take the subway down to the end of Manhattan, and then take the ferry to Staten Island. From there I took a bus to the hospital. I started to think that the apartment was jinxed, since so many things had happened since we moved into it. It was never like this while we lived in the furnished room.

Although I lived at my parents' house, I spend little time there. When I came home from work, I would go to see Nellie in the hospital, and on the weekends, I would go out to Staten

Island to see Robert. In between I went down to lower Manhattan to see Mikey. Even though most of my friends who used drugs hung out right on the corner by my mother's house, I wasn't hanging out too much. I really didn't have too much time to hang out.

My old friend Snazzy was in the air force, and I used to see him from time to time when he came home on leave. He had gotten married while I was still in prison, and his wife had a baby. He was going to be discharged from the air force, and they needed an apartment. I spoke to Nellie, and we had agreed they could use our apartment until they could find a place of their own.

When Snazzy got his discharge, he was trying to find a job. I was on vacation from the eyeglass factory, so I went with him out to New Jersey to apply for a job. We went to a company called Curtis Wright. They made airplane engines, and the pay was good. We were both hired, but I was hired for the night shift. I got a lot of pleasure when I went to my old job to pick up my tools and informed the boss that I would not be returning from my vacation.

While working nights, I wasn't able to visit Nellie during the week. The visiting hours were only at night. My hours were from three p.m. to eleven p.m. Instead, I visited her during the weekends. After about three or four months, I was transferred to days, and everything went back to normal again.

Nellie seemed to be doing fine at the hospital. She had gained some weight, and we were waiting for some doctors to say she was well enough to come home. She would continuously ask the doctors when she would be ready for discharge, but they would never commit themselves. They would just say she was doing fine, but she couldn't go home yet.

One day as I was getting ready to go to the hospital, Nellie called me, and she was hysterical on the phone. I couldn't quite understand what she was upset about. When she calmed down enough to speak clearly, I was able to understand. The doctors wanted to operate on her. They had told her she had to have the operation. After we finished talking, I hung up the phone and rushed to the hospital. As I sat on the bus thinking about what she had just told me, I wondered why they wanted to operate on her now. She had been in the hospital about six months and had made so much progress.

It seemed that the bus caught every red light that day. At last, I got there. When I entered the hospital, I didn't realize that it was still too early to visit. In spite of that, I attempted to go in. A nun stopped me, and when I explained to her that Nellie was very upset, she allowed me to pass. I got to Nellie's room and saw her lying on her bed with her eyes still in tears. When she saw me, she once again started to cry hysterically. I put my arms around her and told her not to worry. It was going to be all right.

Although she never really calmed down completely, we were finally able to talk. She was dead set against having the operation. She was absolutely convinced that she didn't need it. She had seen what the operation had done to other patients, and she didn't want any part of it. I told her that she shouldn't worry; if she didn't want to have it, she didn't have to have it. She even wanted to leave that same night. I convinced her to stay, and we would see how she felt in a few days.

When the visit ended, I left, I went over to a friend's house and got high on drugs. This was a good excuse to get high. I was still using a lot of control and not getting high very often, but on occasion I still did. At that time, I never used a needle to inject myself with drugs. I always inhaled it through my nose. It wasn't that I was afraid of sticking a needle in my arm; I just thought that only a real junkie used a needle, and I wasn't a real junkie. I had a lot of control. I kept telling myself that I would never allow myself to become a junkie. That was for people who had no willpower. There were times that I felt like getting high, but I didn't. I had complete control over it. After all I'd been doing this for over a year and I hadn't gotten hooked yet.

When I got up the next morning to go to work, I wasn't feeling very good. I went to work and felt terrible all day. That night I went to see Nellie, and we talked about what we were going to do. She was still very upset about the operation. We decided that the operation was out. She would be willing to stay in the hospital a little longer, just to make sure that she was all right.

I went home that night and actually prayed to God that she would get completely well. I swore that if he would make her well, I would never use drugs again. I think the last time I prayed was when I went to get sentenced back in 1952. I was very sincere with my plea to God.

Months went by, and I kept my promise. One of the priests in the hospital kept after Nellie because we had not been married in the

Catholic Church. She asked me if I wanted to get married again. I saw that this was important to her and agreed. That year, 1956, we got married on August 15, the same day we had gotten married the first time. It was our second anniversary, and we were getting married again.

After about two months, Nellie started to get real depressed from being in the hospital so long. I thought it was time that she should be coming home. I went to see Snazzy and his wife and told them they should start looking for an apartment. I wanted to give them time to find something nice.

The doctors in the hospital were still trying to get Nellie to accept the operation. She kept refusing, telling them that she didn't need it.

"I'm not going to let you people use me for your experiments," she would tell them.

But they were persistent. Finally, she could not take it anymore. She called me and told me she wanted to leave. I brought her some clothes and took her home. By then Snazzy and his wife had already found another apartment and moved out. The next day Nellie went down to the clinic, and they checked her out. They did all kinds of tests on her and took more x-rays. Everything was fine, they told her. She would have to continue on medication and follow up her appointments.

I brought Mikey home from Nellie's grandmother's house and things started to feel normal. Most weekends we would go to Staten Island to see Robert. He was completely spoiled by the nurses and attendants. When we brought him things to play with, he would break them even before we left. He loved to eat, so we always brought him things to eat. He would eat anything we brought him. It was always an adventure when we went. We would have loved to take him home so we could have him with us. Even Mikey kept asking why we couldn't bring him home. He wanted his brother home so he could play with him.

The factory I was working in started to lay people off. Since I didn't have much time there, I was one of the workers who had to go. Once again, I had to look for a new job and was fortunate to find one right away. It was for less money, but I could work plenty of overtime. I was in charge of operating two small power presses. My job was to set them up to run different kinds of jobs, so it wasn't too boring.

At last, we were able to bring Robert home. He was very hyperactive, and we had our hands full with him. I would come home from work and Nellie would be totally wiped out. Eventually he started to calm down.

I broke my promise and started using drugs again. I found myself getting more and more involved. I had no real reason or excuse: things were doing well for me; the family was all together; Nellie was going well and looking better than she ever did; and we had a lot of good friends whom we socialized with. We would often have parties at our house or at another couple's house. There should have been no reason for me to be doing drugs. It seemed that when things were at their best, I was at my worst. I had my own little world I would escape to.

There were one or two of the guys from our group of friends who would occasionally get high. But sometimes I would go off by myself up to Longwood Avenue to hang out with my old friends. Most of them were already hooked and mainlining. Although I hung out with them, I was still snorting. I was still able to resist putting a needle in my arm.

Nellie was starting to notice the change in me and began to get on my case about it. I was always able to convince her that it wasn't a problem. When she started putting pressure on me, I would slow down for a couple of weeks, but soon I would be at it again. I had even tried to stop completely a few times, but I couldn't stay away very long. I was not physically hooked, but mentally I could not control myself. I realized I was getting high too much and I couldn't do much about it. I was only buying three-dollar bags, but after three or four times a week, it was starting to add up. I was getting deeper and deeper and was not able to stop.

XI

MY UNCLE WILLIE CAME OUT OF prison at that time. I didn't want him to know I was using drugs since he was staying clean. We would visit each other and on occasion, go out partying. I don't think he was aware at first. I wasn't involved with drugs when we were in jail in 1952. I guess he really didn't expect me to do things like that. He had done about four years in Green Haven, and I don't think he planned on doing anything that would cause him to return.

Sometimes we would go up to my parent's house to play a little poker, or we would go to a bar around the corner called the Progresso. A lot of his old crowd hung out at the bar, and we would enjoy hanging out at the place. I knew most of the people there, but they were mainly his crowd. They were about five to ten years older than I was.

Some of them were into selling drugs, and after a while, they asked him if he was interested in doing some dealing. Now these guys weren't junkies. Neither did they want to associate themselves with any junkies; they were in this strictly for the money. They saw that Willie was staying clean and figured they could use someone like him. He knew these guys from the street and had done time with them in jail, so that made him real tight with them.

After thinking about it for a few weeks, Willie and I decided it would be good to have some extra money. We could make a lot if we did things right, so we decided to become partners.

These people were dealing in ounces and kilos. They didn't do business with me; they did it with Willie. I was more familiar with the streets than Willie was. He had the connections.

At first, we were getting just a couple of ounces. The business grew very quickly, and we were almost doubling up every time we picked up a new load. We were spending money like water. I was still getting high on the side. I had so much dope I started to lose control of how much I was using. I was getting high every day. I was sure I was hooked, but since I always had access to dope, I never got sick.

It seemed that we had everybody in the streets selling dope. By then we were only selling quarters. We didn't have to hang out on the corners; the street pushers were the ones out there. Even my old friend Munge was getting heroin from us. He and Carlos, Munge's partner, were dealing and buying a lot of quarters from us.

A number of months went by, and we were still dealing. It was then started to notice how hooked I was. Occasionally when we got rid of all the dope, we had to wait until it was time to pick up a new load. It wouldn't be more than a day or two, but I could feel that for that period of time my body would start to crave drugs. I would have to go out and find some of the pushers who worked for us. If they still had some drugs left, I would borrow some from them. They would always give me something because I always gave them extra when I got my supply.

I was getting paranoid because I knew that at some point, I had to kick this habit. I knew that when that time came, everything would be out in the open. I tried not to think about it.

Although I wasn't out in the street selling drugs directly to the junkies, I had to be careful not to get ripped off. Addicts, I knew, were very desperate people. Killing someone for drugs wasn't uncommon; it happened every day. It wasn't only the addicts I was worried about; it was the police and not getting caught. If the police caught me with such a large amount of drugs, I would be in big trouble.

The pressure was too much for me to bear. Physically, I was rundown. My clothes didn't fit me anymore. My whole system was deteriorating. I was always constipated because heroin did that to me. There was an expression used for someone hooked on drugs, and that is that the person has a monkey on his back. Well, I felt like I had a nine-hundred-pound gorilla on mine.

Another month passed, and I had reached the limit of what I could take. I had to do something about my condition now. It just could not be put off any longer. Something bad was going to happen. I had a couple of close calls, and this had to end. I had already tried to stay off drugs on my own, but it was no use. No matter what I tried, it didn't work. I was trying delay doing anything about it because Christmas was only a month away, but even that couldn't hold me back.

At that time, 1956, hospitals in New York were not treating addicts. There were no treatment programs to go to. You either went to Lexington, Kentucky or you went to Rikers Island for thirty days. That was the choice I had. The United States Public Health Service at Lexington, Kentucky would take much too long. I would have to write a letter and wait for them to answer me. Then I would have to take a physical and have a doctor's letter informing them that I was a drug dependent person.

To go to Rikers Island, all I had to so was to go down to the Tombs in Manhattan and turn myself in. They would take me before a judge, and he would send me to Rikers Island for thirty days. To this day I don't understand how that was done. I'm sure that it wasn't legal. Being an addict was not a crime. At that point I really didn't care whether it was legal or not, I needed it.

Some weeks earlier I had already arranged some time off from my job. That was the easy part; now I had to explain to my parents and Nellie why I was going away. I also had to talk to Willie about it. Willie, being only six years older, was always like a big brother to me. He was a good athlete when he was younger and even tried out for the New York Yankees. He must have impressed them because they wanted to send him to one of their minor league teams. He never reported, but I was never told why. I suspect he might have been already fooling around with drugs, and by the time he had to go; he might have already been too involved.

Willie and I were at a party one night, and I called him into the bathroom where we could talk without being disturbed. I explained to him what I had to do. He was shocked. I guess he didn't realize how bad I was. After he expressed his disappointment in me, he gave me his support.

I spoke to my parents next, and they took it really hard. Everyone became very emotional. I would never have told them if I had known how hard it would be. No one really knew how bad off I was. I don't even think I knew. I had not reached that low level of an addict yet. I didn't have to lie, cheat, or steal for drugs. I only knew what it was to be addicted; I still didn't know what it was to be a junkie.

I stopped dealing a few days before I was to go to Rikers Island. I made sure I had enough dope to hold me until I left. After talking with Nellie, I decided I would leave Monday morning. I had the weekend to prepare myself, so I stayed home with Nellie. It was real nice not having so much pressure on me. It was so good that I started to have second thoughts about leaving on Monday, but my thoughts changed when I remembered I would be running out of heroin by then.

Monday arrived quickly, and once again Nellie and I were saying good-bye. It was a routine we were getting too familiar with, and it was always for the wrong reasons. I kissed her goodbye and headed for the Tombs.

When I arrived, I reported to the office of the court clerk. He called one of the guards, and the guard escorted me to one of the holding pens. Everyone referred to them as bullpens. It would have been no different if I had been arrested for committing a crime. I really didn't care. All I was interested in was doing my thirty days and getting clean.

What happened to me in court that day is unclear. I don't know if it was because it was just so long ago, or if it was because of all the dope I had taken. Before I left the house that morning, I had snorted a very large amount of heroin. I put the remainder in my pocket. Then, when I got off the train, I went into an office building and used the rest of what I had.

Before I realized it, I was on the ferryboat on my way to Rikers Island. The procedure of being processed brought back old memories. This time I knew what to expect. I was going to be there for only thirty days, and I wasn't going to let anything bother me. It was the middle of the afternoon by the time I finally entered the hospital. Hours had gone by, and I still wasn't feeling the slightest bit sick.

There were about eight or nine guys on the ward. When the guard let me in, he said I could take any bed I wanted. All the guys on the ward were there for the same reason; we all had committed ourselves.

It occurred to me later that when you can take a city like New York with thousands and thousands of heroin addicts and less than ten had committed themselves, that should have told me something. But whatever the situation was, I was there for thirty days. There was no way I could leave. I had to deal with it.

By the time it was evening, I was still not feeling any withdrawal. I couldn't understand it. If I had been out in the street, I would have been really sick by this time. I decided it must be because of all the drugs I had taken in the morning.

I slept well for most of the night. It was about four a.m. that I started tossing and turning. It wasn't bad yet, but enough to wake me up. I sat up in my bed and found that most of the other guys were up also. I went over to them and asked if anyone had a cigarette. No one did. They didn't allow anyone to have cigarettes in the hospital. I stayed up with them and joined the conversation. They told me that I had been doing a lot of twisting in bed and they just knew that I would wake up soon.

Some of these guys were real old-timers and had gone through this many times before. I told them that this was my first habit. I continued to explain how long my run was, and how much heroin I was using. They sort of looked at each other in disbelief. I sensed they didn't old believe me. I knew that I was using a lot of heroin, but to them it was unbelievable. If that was the way they thought, (and I knew that what I was saying was true) then kicking this habit was not going to be any picnic.

We continued talking, and as the hours passed by, I could feel myself getting worse. My legs were bothering me more than anything else. It seemed that the pain was coming from deep down in the bones. Nothing I did made the pain go away or even feel better. I had other symptoms, too. One was an annoying feeling in my throat. It was not painful, but it would affect whatever I ate. Occasionally it would make me nauseous. I had no appetite at all.

We talked until the sun came up, then we were told to line up for breakfast. The hot cereal made me feel like throwing up. I could only drink the coffee. The pain in my legs was now spreading to my lower back.

After breakfast we were taken back to the ward. I kept going to the bathroom to urinate, but that was all I could do. I was constipated, and that was bothering me.

The only thing we could do to kill time was talk. It was like an ongoing conversation. Sometimes we would get up and go to our beds to lie down. When we got tired of tossing and turning, we would return to the group. Someone else would get up and walk up and down the ward, then return. It went on that way all day.

As the day progressed, the sicker I became. I couldn't eat lunch or dinner. I was only able to take the liquids.

One of the men in our group was the type of person who stood out from all the others, a real character you could never forget. He was an older guy who had been using drugs for over twenty years. We would all sit around him and listen to his stories. He said he was forty-five years old, but I was sure that he was not telling the truth. He told us how he used to buy his drugs in the drugstores. I found his stories hard to believe at times, but that didn't matter. He had been all over the country and told us how drug laws were so different in each place. He reminisced over the years of the Depression and how he went from state to state in railroad cars. Said he slept in hobo camps and would wander into the small towns to ask for food.

"Drugs were so cheap that I didn't even have to steal," he said one time. "I could go into a drugstore, and for less than a dollar, buy enough to last a week."

No matter how sick I was, he would always help me keep my mind off how I felt. Occasionally I would get cigarettes from some of the prisoners I knew who were working in the hospital. I don't remember the old-timer's name, but whenever I had cigarettes, he was sure to stay up with me. When the old man left the hospital, I really missed him.

Seven days went by, and after the third day, I began feeling better with each passing day. After the nurse thought we were well enough, we would be sent to one of the cellblocks for the rest of the thirty days. I still wasn't well enough but thought how it would be better to be out there than in the hospital.

About ten days after I had been admitted to the ward, I convinced the nurse I was feeling good enough to leave. After expressing some doubts, she finally agreed, and I was let out of the hospital. I still wasn't sleeping, but I was eating a lot better.

When I hit the cellblock, I just kept greeting people I knew. All the guys there were doing time. On Rikers Island no one did more than three years; most were just doing six months or a year. Personally, I felt that I was on vacation. I had only about twenty days left and didn't even think much about that. Fortunately, there was one man to a cell. Since I couldn't sleep yet, I didn't have to worry about keeping anyone up.

After two weeks I was eating like a horse. I'm sure I gained a few pounds each day. When I went to the commissary, I bought everything I could. If I was going to stay up all night in my cell, I was going to have enough to eat and smoke.

After three weeks, I was starting to get some catnapping in. I still was awake for most of the night, but each night after I would sleep a little more. It was the Christmas week, and I thought of the time in Coxacki when I told my boss I would never spend another Christmas in jail. Well, it didn't matter; I would be home in about a week anyway.

XII

1957 STARTED OUT RIGHT; I WAS clean and I was on my way home. I think it was either January second or third. The holidays were over, and there seemed to be a calm in the air. I didn't live very far from where the ferry dropped us off. It was only about a fifteen-minute bus ride.

I got home early, and the first thing I did when I got in the house was wake Nellie. We greeted each other with an embrace. She was very surprised to see how much weight I had gained. The kids woke up, and I was so glad to see them. We were together, just the four of us, and we had a great day.

Later we went to my parents' house. They spent most of the time giving me advice, especially my mother. When we returned home, some friends had come over. Everything was nice, and I didn't have to do my usual disappearing act. We had a few drinks and listened to some records. It felt good, not wanting to get high on drugs. None of my friends who had come over were into any drugs, so it didn't even come up.

I stayed home a couple of days and then went down to my old job. I should have used the opportunity to look for another job, but I figured I would try them first.

As soon as I walked in the door, my boss said, "It's good to see you, Miguel. When will you be ready to return to work?"

I didn't have much of a chance to think about it, so I said, "Tomorrow morning, if it's okay with you."

I went to the office to make sure my timecard was in the rack. Then I went to my locker to check my work clothes. I started to place the dirty clothing in a bag to take home. As I looked through the pockets, I felt some papers, and when I pulled then out, I saw that I had a quarter-ounce bag of heroin in my hand. I felt shock waves go through me.

One of the other workers came toward me, so I pushed the bag of dope back into the pocket. He greeted me with his hand out. I had just enough time to pull my hand out of the pocket to meet his. I explained that I would be at work, and he told me he was glad to see me back. I couldn't hold much of a conversation with him because all I could think of was that bag of dope. After about two minutes, I shook his hand again and told him that I had to leave.

As I walked to catch the subway home, all that was going through my mind was the quarter bag of dope. I was trying to think of when I could have left it in my pocket. How could I have forgotten about it? What was more important was what was I going to do with it? This was the third day since I had come home. I was clean and didn't have any physical need to use any dope.

When I got up that morning, I had no intention or urge to get high, but now here I was on my way home with a bag of dope. I could just sell it for twenty-five dollars, or I could make up bags and sell them for fifty dollars . . . or I could use it to get high on.

I changed trains at Fourteenth Street. It occurred to me that I could get high right then. Then I reminded myself that all that suffering I had gone through would be wasted if I got high now. Everything I had planned to do would go down the drain. And how would Nellie feel if she found out that I got high again?

The roar of the express train interrupted my thoughts. It screeched to a stop, the doors opened, and I got in. As the doors closed behind me, I resumed thinking about the dope. The thought of throwing it away left me as quickly as it came. If I used it, I could use it just this time. After all, I didn't go out looking to get high. It wasn't costing me any money, Deep down I knew what I was thinking was wrong, but that was how I wanted to think. I was going to get high, and I had to convince myself that it was something I could handle.

What will become of me if I get strung out again? I wondered, Finally I told myself, "the hell with it!" "Just one time won't hurt." I looked up and saw that we were pulling away from Thirty-fourth Street. (As I look at it now, all that thinking took place between Fourteenth Street and Thirty-fourth Street. Probably a five- or six-minute ride. That's how long it took to convince myself to give in to the urge.) The next stop was Forty-second Street. As the train was slowing down, I was already thinking of where I could go to snort down the dope.

The doors of the train opened, and I was headed for the first bathroom I could find. The first one I found didn't have any doors in the stalls so I couldn't do it there. The next bathroom was just fine. It was the kind where you have to put a dime in the meter to use it. I went into the stall and locked the door behind me. I sat on the toilet and looked for the pocket that had the dope. When I found it, I laid the bag of dirty clothes over to the far corner of the stall. I opened the glassine bag and thought for a second about what I was going to do with what I couldn't use. It was too much dope to snort up on one high. I reached into my pocket and pulled out a book of matches, tore off a strip, and formed it into a small scoop. I then burrowed the scoop into the heroin and moved it around to fluff it up. (It was easier to scoop up that way.) Finally, I brought the scoop filled with heroin up to my nose and snorted it up. That bitter taste shot threw my head. So bitter, but so sweet.

I wondered how much I should take. I was clean and didn't know how much I could use now. I had never heard of anyone dying from an overdose from snorting, but I thought it might be possible. I snorted about six scoops. There was still a lot of heroin left in the bag, more than half. I closed it up, reached for the bag of clothes, and returned the heroin to the same pocket it had been in. I reached for some toilet paper and cleaned my nose, so no traces of the drug remained visible.

I sat there about a minute, thinking of what I had done. If only I hadn't found that bag of dope in my work clothes. Now what am I going to do with the rest of the dope? I should throw it away. Maybe I should flush it down the toilet. I'll just hold on to it for a while. Let's see how the amount I took is going to make me feel. If I don't feel good enough, I could take some more before I throw the rest away.

I opened the door to the stall and walked out of the bathroom. As I got back on the train, I started to feel the heroin having its effect on me. I tried not to nod on the train, but it was no use. I had to change trains again at 125th Street. I just made it. Getting off on Longwood Avenue was no easy task either, but I made that too.

The cold air hit me as I walked up the stairway of the train station. I realized I couldn't go home in this condition. Nellie would be terribly disappointed in me, and besides that, she would get on my case. I knew I would not be able to fool her. She practically always knew when I was high.

I decided not to go home yet, so I walked up Longwood Avenue to Dawson Street. If I hung around while my high would go down and I could go home. I went into a candy store and Longwood where a lot of my old dope-fiend friends hung out. Some of the guys who had been selling dope for me were hanging out in the candy store.

"Hey, Miguel, you back in business?" they asked when they saw me.

I couldn't stay there very long. All these people were hanging out in the candy store, just waiting for something to happen. Eventually someone came around looking to buy drugs or needing a set of works. They knew they would always find that someone in the candy store who could help them.

I still didn't see myself as a street junkie. Not only that, but I still had some dope in the bag of clothes. I left the candy store and kept going up Longwood Avenue. I thought of going to a movie. That would be good for a few hours. On my way up to the movies, I went into one of the buildings on Longwood Avenue. I walked all the way up to the area that entered the roof. I took out my bag of dope and started to get high again. I had taken about two or three blows out of it when I heard some noise come from the floor below. My first thought was that it might be the police. I stood absolutely still, trying to listen for another sound. If it were the police, they would have already pounced on me.

I started to fold up the bag of dope, trying to be as quiet as possible. After folding it, I leaned over very slowly, trying to look down to the floor below. After leaning out as far as I could, all I saw was two pairs of shoes. I couldn't lean any further without falling so I leaned back. Judging from the condition of the shoes, I knew they didn't belong to cops.

It must be a couple of junkies, I guess. They must have thought I was going to hide some drugs on the roof.

I put the drugs back in the pants, and I just threw the pants carelessly toward the corner opposite the door that led to the roof. I was sure they weren't going to try to stick me up because they would have already approached me.

I turned toward the stairway and started down. There they were, with a surprised look on their faces. They weren't prepared for me to come down. They must have figured I would go out through the roof. I knew both of them. They weren't what I considered friends; I just knew them because they were part of the drug world.

I saw that they were both in need of a fix.

"What are you guys doing here?" I asked when I reached them. After some hesitation, the tall thin one spoke up. "We were casing one of the apartments on the floor below. When we heard someone coming up the stairs, we came up here."

It was easy to see that they were lying. If they actually were afraid like they said, they would have gone all the way up to where I was.

I put the whole incident aside. I thought about the quarter I had in the pants pocket. I was only an eight by now. This was my chance to get rid of it.

"Do you guys have any money?" I asked.

It was a dumb question. If they had money, they wouldn't be here. What I really wanted to do was get rid of the dope so I could go home.

The short, unshaven one said, "We aren't feeling so good. If you can give us something, we'll pay you later."

I said okay, knowing damn well they would never pay me. I turned and went back up to the top landing. I nodded for them to follow, and they did. I picked up the pants and took the dope out of the pocket.

They looked at each other in surprise. I handed them the dope and started to put the pants back in the bag.

"Have you got any works on you?" the thin one asked.

"No," I told them.

"We don't have any either," he replied. Then he got an idea. "Let's go over to my house. We can use my stuff."

I should have let them go by themselves, but for some strange reason, I wanted to go with them. I couldn't understand my feeling then, and I still don't know if I understand them now. These were two dope fiends who had given up all their respectability. They didn't care what anyone thought of them, and in spite of all that, I wanted to go with them. I was finding some satisfaction in lowering myself down to their level, degrading myself, and I didn't know why. It was like I had a need to do that.

I took the bag of dope back from the guy I had handed it to and said, 'All right, let's go."

Although I went with them, I didn't want to be seen walking together with them. I kept about a half block distance behind them. After about four or five blocks, they paused in front of a beat-up old building, looked back to be sure I was still behind them, and then entered.

As I passed through the entrance, I had to step over the piles of garbage on the floor. One of the guys was waiting for me at the top of the stairs. There was no light in the hall, and since it had started to get dark outside, it was hard to see. I reached the first floor and very carefully followed him up to the next floor. On the way it occurred to me that this must be a condemned building since only a few apartments appeared to be occupied.

On the second floor we entered into one of the apartments. The unshaven one closed the door and then picked up a two-by-four that was leaning on the wall behind the door. There was another piece of two-by-four nailed to the floor. He then placed the first piece between the door and the wood on the floor. It was all done so smoothly I could not help but be amazed. Judging from the condition of the apartment, I was certain the two-by-four wasn't meant to keep out burglars.

We walked through the kitchen and what I guessed was the living room. We entered the rear bedroom, and one of them opened a closet and took out his works. They were in a package of cigarettes. Before I realized it, he had them out on the floor. It seemed that everything was on the floor. The room had no light, so he lit a few candles.

Just then the other guy walked into the room carrying a bottle of water. The guy on the floor reached out and asked me for the stuff. I was already carrying it in my hand, just in case I had to get rid of it. By this time, he had all the works laid out on the floor. He had an eyedropper, a needle, and a couple of bottle caps, one bigger than the other. I handed him the bag of dope.

"Should I cook up the whole bag?" he asked.

"Yes," I told him, suddenly aware that I included myself in this.

In spite of the fact that I had gotten high twice that day, I was now going to get high again. But this time it was going to be by putting a needle into my vein. I had never even taken a skin pop, and here I was, getting ready to mainline.

He emptied the whole bag into the big bottle cap and measured three equal eyedroppers of water. He had already put the heroin into the bottle cap that was called the cooker. With his fingers, he held the cooker over one of the candles. I wondered why he didn't get burned. It only took a few second for the water to boil. Once it boiled, he removed it from the flame of the candle and placed the needle into the cooker. In the bottom of the cooker was a small piece of cotton. With the eyedropper that was attached to the needle, he drew up the first shot. He turned in my direction, handing me the shot. I froze because I wasn't ready for this.

"You go first," I told him.

I held the shot so he could get ready. He took his jacket off one arm, and in a second, had his belt around it. He pulled the belt tight and held it in place by bracing his knee up against it. I could see the place he was going to use. He had this long dark track that ran down his forearm; it was about six inches long. The end of the track looked raw. He placed the needle in that spot and tapped the eyedropper with his index finger. The needle entered his skin, and a thick stream of blood entered the eyedropper. He then squeezed the heroin and blood mixture into the vein. Immediately he reacted with a sigh of satisfaction. The whole procedure was done with a sort of religious feeling--more or less a ritual. Maybe it was the candles and the silence that gave that atmosphere.

The second guy took the needle and flushed water through it. He drew up his shot, and once again performed the same ceremony. Now it was my turn, and I knew that I couldn't do this on my own. I removed just one arm from my jacket, and with the guy's belt, I managed to wrap it around my arm myself. I became afraid when I saw the amount that was still left in the cooker. When I drew it up, I squirted some back into the cooker. I knew I couldn't take the same amount that these guys took. I handed the works to the guy who had gotten off first.

"Where do you want me to hit you?" he asked.

"Wherever you think is best," I told him.

The needle entered, and again the blood came up through the heroin, only this time it was my blood. Then I could feel that warm rush go through my entire body, a feeling that cannot be explained. If was a good thing I had put some back because I probably would have taken an overdose.

The high I was on lasted for hours. I prayed to God to get me down. No matter where I stopped, I would go into a nod.

Finally, I started to feel in control of myself. I was still in the area of the building, but I didn't know what had happened to the two guys I was with. I started walking home and thinking about what had happened.

When I finally got home, Nellie immediately knew I was high on drugs.

She yelled, "You haven't been out of the hospital a week yet and already you have to use drugs."

I tried denying it, but it was no use. She yelled, screamed, and cried. I just sat on the living room couch, not saying a word. There wasn't much I could say. I had no answers for her. I had no answers for myself. I still had no reason that I could understand.

The children were in another room playing. They were not concerned with any of this. I went into the room they were in and sat down next to where they were playing, but it was no use. They were playing a game called Operation. Certain organs of the body had to be placed in the proper part of the body. If they weren't careful putting it in place, a buzzer of some kind would go off and they would lose their turn. I attempted it without success. I told my son Mikey that this game was too hard for them to play. I picked him up and started playing with him. I threw him on the bed, and then Robert jumped me from behind. I fell on the floor as if he had knocked me down. Before I knew it, they were both on top of me. I begged for them to have mercy on me. The more I begged, the more they would beat on me.

Mikey was four and Robert was about two years of age. I don't think they understood much at the time. Their world was different from mine. I wished that I could go back to their world.

We rolled over, and now I was on top of them. They kept swinging their arms, and again we rolled over. Now they were on top. Just then Nellie came into the room and said it was past their bedtime. Mikey's protest did no good. I left the room while Nellie put them to bed. I was watching TV when she came into the living room and sat down. She wanted to know what I was going to do.

"I'm sorry, Nellie. I promise you it'll never happen again. I made this one mistake, but it's the last time."

I then explained how I had found the bag of dope in my work clothes.

"What happened to the clothes?" she asked.

I had completely forgotten what I did with the bag.

After some hesitation, I said, "I must have left it in that place I got high at. Well, I'm not going back there to get them. There's no way I'm going to do that again."

And this time I really meant it. I was sincere in what I had promised. I would go to work the next day, and when I came home, I was going to stay home—no going out and no drugs.

XIII

MY ADDICTION CONTINUED FOR SEVEN MORE years. During that of time I was not able to get off drugs for any significant amount of time. We went through a lot of depression, especially Nellie. She tried desperately to keep everything together, but it was an impossible task. Her only break was when I was either in jail or in some hospital taking a cure.

Fortunately, she had some good friends, such as Elsie. Elsie was married to Nellie's cousin Tony, but they had been friends from their early teens. No matter how bad things were, Elsie would always come over to visit Nellie. Although Nellie had other friends who visited her on occasion, it was Elsie who never stopped. Her life was similar to Nellie's in that they were both teenage mothers. They went through lot together and were able to help each other through the hard times.

In 1959 we had another child, Steven Alexander. He was born during the worst of times. I was using all the money I could get my hands on to shoot dope. Things had gone from bad to worse. Nellie's grandmother used to come all the way from lower Manhattan to bring food for her and the kids. I could never understand how she managed to come all that distance with those shopping bags. She would usually get there before we got up in the morning. She would bang on the door until we got up. When we opened the door, she would march herself right into the apartment and start picking up and putting things in place. I would avoid her. It made me feel guilty that this woman would come all that distance because I was not able to take care of my family. I would usually wake up, get dressed, and leave the house.

I was out of the house most of the time. At night I would roam the streets, looking to break into cars. I would steal all sorts of things, but mostly I would take the spare tire. That was always good for a sure fix. I had a lot of close calls because sometimes the owners would see me. They would come charging out of their house to catch me. When that happened, I would run with whatever I had. If they would come close to catching me, I would drop whatever I had taken from their car. That would always stop them.

I would get involved with anything I could to get money for drugs, but I was always careful not to get involved with anything major. I didn't want to go back to prison and do a lot of time. I never went in for cashing checks or anything that required a gun. I would only do petty crimes. That way, if I got caught, I would only have to do short bids like ninety days or six months.

It went on and on for those seven years, from Lexington, Kentucky to Metropolitan Hospital. From Rikers Island to Harts Island. From Manhattan General Hospital to Manhattan State Hospital.

I even had a job as a machine operator. I could never understand how they put up with me. I worked there for about four years, on and off. Every time I got myself cleaned up, I would call them, and they would always give me my job back. I would work until I got hooked again or got arrested.

In 1960 we moved from 156th Street up to Clifton Avenue around 181st. There weren't very many other Puerto Ricans around there, but no one bothered us. It didn't help my addiction much. There wasn't much around there as far as drugs was concerned. I would have to take the bus downtown to the old neighborhood to buy drugs. The one good thing was that I did better at breaking into cars. The people seemed to be more careless with their vehicles in this area.

Each year was basically a repeat of the previous year. I continued to put Nellie through the same thing, and she had just about had enough. Somehow, I was able to convince her that I was going to change, but I never did. Each broken promise would take a little more out of her until she had nothing left to give.

It must have been in early 1963 when she decided to leave me.

She went down to see a social worker at family relations. She not only wanted to leave me, but she wanted it in the form of a legal separation. I was supposed to go with her to see the worker. I went once, but I didn't go back.

At first, I had agreed to let her have the legal separation, but later I found I could not bring myself to accept it. I knew what I was doing to her and the kids, and I didn't want my children to have to be deprived of what other kids had, but I could not control myself. I had an uncontrollable desire to use drugs. I didn't want it that way, but I could not do anything to stop. It was almost like a disease. I wanted desperately to get away from having to use drugs, but I couldn't. I didn't know how.

Sometimes when I got up in the morning, I would say to myself that I wasn't going to go out. I would try to keep my mind occupied with anything I could. Eventually, the urge got too powerful. Even if I didn't have any money or any means of getting money, I still would go out looking to get some dope. What I wouldn't do for any other reason, I would do for drugs.

Now I was about to lose my wife. In this world there was nothing that I loved more than Nellie. She was my only hope, and I couldn't let her go. I was afraid that without her I wouldn't even try to get off. And what would I do without my children? Mikey, the oldest, was already = ten years old. In spite of my sickness, I was close to them. They knew they had a father who loved them, but they also knew that something was wrong with him.

As this crisis got worse, so did my addiction. I didn't want to think about it. More drugs made it easier. That was my way of solving everything.

Nellie kept telling me she wanted me to leave. I kept telling her I would, but I knew I wasn't going to. That didn't help at all.

Where was I going to go? If I left, I would have to sleep in a basement or on a rooftop somewhere. I just could not see myself doing that.

Months passed, and nothing changed. I would leave the house during the day and return at night. I had no set hours for either leaving or returning home. Sometimes I wouldn't get home until the next day.

It must have been in either late October or early November of 1963 that Nellie finally could not take any more. She packed up the kids and left.

It took me awhile to understand that she was gone. I had come home early that particular day and called out for Nellie. When she didn't answer, I looked around and realized what had happened. It was almost more than I could bear. I didn't want to be alone in the apartment, so I went out and started walking. I'm not sure how far I walked, but soon it was daylight. I stopped to rest on some steps leading up to an apartment building. A man walked by with his lunch in a paper bag. His clothes were shabby, and I knew he didn't have much. Still, I remember thinking that I would gladly change places with him. Even if I had to live the rest of my life with nothing more than he had.'

Nine years had passed since I first started using drugs, and I had reached the bottom. I remembered the two junkies I was with the first time I shot dope. I remembered that I didn't even want to walk down the street with them. Now I had reached that level. I wondered how many people wouldn't walk down the street with me. I could not live with that feeling. I never felt like killing myself, and I couldn't think of doing anything like that even then, but I just couldn't go on like that.

I sat there a while longer. Some guy pulled up in front of where I was sitting. He double-parked his car and honked his horn.

He must be picking somebody up for work. I thought.

No one responded, and he honked the horn again. After a couple of minutes, he got out of the car and went into the building. I watched him secure the car before he left. He reached across and pushed down the locks on both the front and rear door. I noticed that he didn't check the rear door on the driver's side. I could see that the lock looked higher than the rest.

The man rushed into the building, and I got up to look in the car. I tried the rear door, and it was open. I reached in and pulled out a suitcase and a large paper bag that were in the rear seat. I didn't check anything else, because I knew the guy would be right out. I closed the door to the car and walked down the street with the suitcase and bag. I wanted to go away from the scene as fast as possible, but at the same time, I had to walk as casual as I could. I didn't want the cops to stop me.

The stress became too much for me, so I ducked into one of the building and went all the way up to the roof. I went over to edge of the roof and looked over. I saw the man open the front door of the car, get in, and drive off. He didn't even notice the stuff was gone.

Feeling relieved, I opened the paper bag to see what I had stolen. The bag was filled with films, a 35mm camera, and an 8mm movie projector. All I cared about was that it would be enough to feed my habit.

Within a half hour, I had sold the camera for twenty-five dollars. I bought some dope and was on my way home to get high.

After I shot some of the dope, I checked out the films. I had suspected they might be pornographic films, and I was right. I put them aside to check them out later.

I got sick from the high. When the sickness wore off I began to feel the results of having stayed up all night so I lay down on the bed and fell asleep. After a few hours I awakened and remembered I still had some dope, so I shot up again. It was already late in the afternoon, and I started to think of how I was going to get rid of the films and projector. I also thought of going down to Nellie's mother's house to see if she was there.

I made some coffee, which was all there was in the house. But that was okay; I had a half load of dope, about fifteen three-dollar bags, and that was all that mattered.

When I finished the coffee, I decided I would go see if I could find Nellie. I hid the dope and the works, left the house, and took the bus downtown.

Nellie's mother lived on Eagle Avenue near 149th Street. While on the bus, I remembered a guy I knew who liked to buy a lot of stolen goods. He lived on Prospect Avenue. I decide to go there first.

I got off the bus near my friend's house and went to see him. I tried to get two hundred and fifty dollars for the films and projector. He said he would only give me fifty. After negotiating for a little while, we settled for a hundred. He drove me back to my house, and we made the deal.

I took another shot of dope before I once again left for Nellie's mother's house. When I got there, I knocked on the door, but no one answered. Her mother lived on the ground floor, so I went outside and tried looking through the window. It had gotten dark outside, but I couldn't see any lights. Maybe she and the kids were in there and she didn't want to see me. I went back and stood close to the door to listen for any movement inside. I heard nothing. I knew her mother was always home, especially this time of day. I imagined that they were all huddled in one of the rooms, waiting for me to go away.

I took the bus back uptown. I couldn't wait to go back home to take some more dope. I had enough for a day or two and money to buy more, but I wasn't feeling much better. I got high because I had to. At this point, it wasn't something that I could enjoy. I was feeling down and lonely. I had often felt this way, but I think that at this point I was at my lowest. I was not only destroying myself, but also my family.

I looked around at the people on the bus. Some were going home from work; others were going to visit family or friends; some were going or coming from shopping. They were all doing something normal. How I wished my life was like theirs. Once again, I thought of the man, I had seen early that morning, the one going to work with the paper bag. Why can't I live like that? Why was my life different? I hated them because they had control of their lives. I hated myself because I couldn't be like them. If only I could change. I didn't want to live like this. The people

I loved didn't want to be with me anymore.

I have to do something to change all this, I told myself. I have to go into some hospital and kick this habit. If I don't, it will be too late.

XIV

IN THE PAST WHEN I GOT off the bus at night, I would pick up a pizza and some soda and go home. That was one of the few events that brought a little joy to Nellie and the kids. Nellie knew that when I brought something like that home, I would also have some money to give her. Although I hadn't eaten all day, I really bought the pizza because it related to a good feeling.

Now when I walked into the house, I realized that the pizza wasn't going to help. I laid the box on the kitchen table and went into the bathroom to get my works and dope. I would always get high in the bathroom, but today I went into the kitchen. I put three bags into the cooker and put my last three bags on the side. I shot the three bags into my arm and put everything away.

With a slice of pizza and a glass of soda, I sat in front of the TV set and nodded myself away. I would get up once in a while for one reason or another. After a while I laid on the bed and fell asleep.

I got up at about three a.m. and took a shower and changed clothes. I Then I shot up the rest of the dope. I ate another slice of pizza (cold this time), put the box in the refrigerator, and was on my way downtown to get more dope and try to find Nellie.

After having taken care of everything in that order, I found myself once again standing in front of Nellie's mother's apartment, trying to listen through the door. It must have been around 7:00 a.m. I knocked on the door and listened again. I heard some movement in the apartment, so I knocked again.

I heard a kid ask, "Who is it?"

I answered, and the door opened. It was one of my mother-in-law's kids. I acted very casual as I asked him if Nellie was there.

He looked at me with wide eyes and said, "Yes."

I walked into the living room, sat down on the couch, and waited for the rest of my family to wake up. I had a half load of dope in my pocket and about sixty dollars.

My mother-in-law got up first, saw me in the living room, said hello, and the disappeared into the kitchen. Next it was Stevie. When he saw me, he came running and hopped up onto my lap. He had just turned four and was the baby of the house.

I was talking to him, and when I looked up, Nellie was standing in the doorway that led to the living room. She looked at me a moment and then went into the bathroom without saying a word. She wanted to see if I was high or sick. I knew that look so well.

The other kids had gotten up by now, and they were all in the living room when Nellie came out of the bathroom. She sent them into the bathroom to wash up.

She sat across from me and asked, "How did you know I was here?"

"I wasn't sure. I just took the chance. Were you here yesterday when I came by?"

"Yes."

"Why didn't you open the door and talk to me?"

"Miguel, I'm not ready yet. I need to think things over."

"Well, what are we going to do?" I asked.

She looked away. "I don't know what I'm going to do. I just know I can't live like this anymore. I don't think anything is ever going to change. Year in and year out, things just never get better. I just can't take it anymore. I've tried so hard for us to stay together, hoping that you would change, but things just get worse. I tried getting a separation so I could at least get on welfare."

"I know that someday you'll change. That's what keeps me going. You're a good man, Miguel, but you're weak. I don't know what makes a person have to use drugs, but it doesn't affect just you. It made me and the children suffer along with you. Just look at the way we have to live. We don't have anything left. Even our old friends don't come around to visit. You have to do something, or I'm just going to go crazy."

She could not hold back the tears from her eyes.

Just then Mikey came into the room, and she sent him for a tissue. I got up from where I was sitting and sat next to her. I put my arms around her, and she buried her head in my chest. Her sobs were heavy, and she could not talk. By then the boys had come into the room to see why their mommy was crying. Stevie climbed up on her lap and put his arms around her. I reached out for Mikey and Robert. We were all huddled on the couch, crying together. No one said a word. No yelling, no accusations. No one was blaming me. It was a time to fight back.

"This disease is not going to destroy us," I vowed, "We'll fight this until we beat it."

In the nine years that I used drugs, I could not remember ever having such a strong desire to stop. I looked into her eyes.

"Nellie, I'm not going to make the kind of promises that I always made and didn't keep. This time I'll show you. We won't let this destroy us. We've suffered enough."

We started gathering all the things that she had taken. I spoke with Nellie's mother and told her about what we had decided. She always gave me encouragement. I was grateful.

When we got home, we talked more about our plans. I gave Nellie the dope I had and the works. We agreed that she was going to give me a bag only when it was absolutely necessary. She put it away, and then we went shopping. I had already given her the sixty dollars that I had. She must have spent around fifty dollars in the supermarket. (In 1963 you could get a lot of groceries for fifty dollars, and we had to pay extra to have them deliver all that food.)

We spent the rest of the afternoon putting the food away and straightening up the house. In the evening I made plans with Nellie. I would go down to see if I could get into Metropolitan Hospital. She would go down and apply for welfare until I came home. Then I would go back to work, and no more dope. We would be able to do all the things we had not done for so many years.

The next morning, I got up early, and after Mikey and Robert went off to school, I got myself ready to go down and start the procedure of getting into the hospital. Nellie gave me a bag of dope, and I shot it before I left. I didn't get high off the bag, but it did keep me from getting sick.

When I got down to the hospital, I discovered it wasn't going to be easy. The waiting list to get in was long, and I was told it would take about a month before I could get in. Another guy who was there told me it was like that all over. He then told me about a church in the Bronx that was helping addicts. I had heard about that place before, but I didn't think I wanted to go there. I had seen some of the guys who had gone there walking around with Bibles under their arms. They would hold street services on the corners where the addicts hung out and preach to them. I considered them fanatics. I didn't want to get involved with them.

When I got home, I told Nellie about what had happened. We agreed that if I couldn't find anything right away, I should try the church.

The next day I went to another hospital and ran into the same problem. On my way home I decided to stop at the church. I was surprised to find so many guys I knew living right there in the building the church was in. they appeared to be serious about giving their lives to Christ. Even though I wasn't sure I wanted to do this, I must admit that I was impressed with the people there. I wasn't sure if it was my need to get clean, but I found myself wanting what these people had.

They were all getting set for this big Thanksgiving dinner and service that they had every year. It was for all the addicts, alcoholics, and homeless. They would have a Thanksgiving dinner and then a service.

When I got home, I told Nellie that maybe I should try it out. I knew I had to do something. Thanksgiving was only about a week away. I had gotten this flyer and I showed it to Nellie. It explained all about the dinner and the service that would follow.

I didn't have enough dope to hold me until Thanksgiving, so I had to go out a couple of times. I also went to the church a couple of times during the week to make sure they were aware of me. They had a camp upstate where they sent all the new people. It was called the Christian Youth Crusade.

During that week I cut down on my habit to show Nellie how serious I was. She was giving me three bags a day now. It was enough to hold me, but barely.

On one of my visits to the church I was presented to the directors of the program. I really shouldn't use the word program; everything was so different from all the hospitals I had been in. most of the people were warm and would talk to you with more concern. There were no doctors or nurses. You wouldn't get any medication here. All anyone said was that Jesus changed their lives.

The residents did everything—the cooking as well as the cleaning. I wasn't really a resident at the time. I would first have to go up to the camp in Mountaindale, New York and stay there until I was ready. There was no time period that I would have to stay there. I would stay for as long as it took.

Although the program was supported by a group of churches, it wasn't doing very well financially. But no one seemed to care. The solution to any problem was always, "The Lord will provide." I was feeling very good with the people there, and actually I couldn't wait to go to the camp.

The founder of the Christian Youth Crusade was Reverend Francisco Rosado and his wife Reverend Leoncia Rosado. Everyone referred to her as mama Leo. She was a warm woman who would always find the time to listen, but also had a way about her that was strong and sure. I felt safe when she was around. It was like she could handle any situation. When she spoke to me, she gave me the impression that she could tell if I was lying. Even though I had spoken with them only a couple of times, it was enough for me to already feel that way.

Thanksgiving day finally arrived. Although I didn't go to church to have dinner, I wanted to be there for the service. I got there late, and the service was almost over. I walked up one flight to the chapel. It seemed that everyone was screaming and yelling. Some were dancing in the spirit and others were speaking in tongues. I had been to a lot of Pentecostal services when I was younger with my grandmother, but I had never been to one like this. It really got me frightened. I didn't understand what was going on. I looked around, and no one else looked like they were afraid of what was happening. I didn't want to leave because then I would lose the opportunity of going to Mountaindale. I couldn't let that happen now. I would go through with this no matter what.

I looked up on the pulpit and saw that I knew the preacher. He was an ex-drug addict from Wales Avenue. His name was Joe, I knew, because his name came up all the time. He had been the first addict to come to the church. I had heard that God was using him to preach to the addict and alcoholic. Well, he was really used today. Everyone was really affected by his sermon. He stood on the pulpit, holding the microphone with one hand and waving his other hand as if inviting the people to come forward. I knew that if I was going to go to Mountaindale, I had better get up there. It wasn't going to be easy from where I was.

I took a deep breath and started for the pulpit. The alter was crowded, and I could not get very close. Someone put their arm around me and started to pray for me. I was asked if I wanted to accept the Lord as my personal Savior, and I said yes. With an arm still around me, the man managed to position me right in front of the pulpit. I really felt moved by what was happening. Before I realized it, I was holding my arms straight up in the air. The person with me kept encouraging me to ask the lord to help me.

"Help me, Lord," I said in a low voice.

As I repeated it, my voice grew louder and louder until I was shouting it out, "help me, lord!"

After about ten or fifteen minutes, things calmed down, and Joe started speaking in a lower voice. He said over and over, "Seek and you shall find. All things are possible if you seek."

I looked at Joe and saw that he was soaked with perspiration. I didn't know Joe very well while he was a dope fiend, but I knew who he was. I knew that he was an addict to the core. I never would have thought that he would be preaching the gospel of Jesus Christ. It was inspiring for me to see that.

In the programs that I had gone to in the past, I never saw anyone who could really stay clean like Joe. Even the guys I had seen preaching in the street were staying off drugs. My way of looking at it was that I didn't care what it took; I just wanted to stop using drugs.

After the service ended and all the members of the church had gone home, I stayed, along with about twenty other people who had also accepted Christ. Most of us were dope addicts and alcoholics, but we were mostly drug addicts. I was hoping they would take us up to the camp that very night. We sat there in the empty church waiting to find out what was going to happen next. I think that most of us were thinking about the same thing, but not in the same way.

I heard someone saying that he hoped they were not thinking of sending him up to the camp tonight. After he said that, I could tell from the comments that followed that most were in agreement. But I was ready to go right then and there. My fear was that they would not take us.

Just then someone came into the chapel and invited us downstairs, When we went down, we had coffee and some cookies. After that was over, some of the ex-addicts spoke to us about how accepting Christ had changed their lives. I was very impressed with what they said. That was what I wanted. I didn't care what I had to do, just so I could stop using drugs. If it meant walking around with a Bible and preaching on corners, I was more than willing to do it.

They asked if anyone had any questions. I raised my hand.

"Are we going up to Mountaindale tonight?" I asked.

They replied, "No, not tonight, because we don't have any transportation, but we hope we can get someone by tomorrow. Those of you who wish to go will have to come back then. We don't have enough room to let you all stay here tonight, so those who have a place to stay can go there. We will try to find something for the rest of you."

It was not what I wanted to hear. I didn't want to go back home. First of all, I didn't have any money or dope. I knew I was going to get sick. I didn't want to have to go out stealing, not tonight, not on the night that I accepted Christ as my Savior. Although I knew within me that I was doing all this for the wrong reasons, I still felt that making that decision was important.

It was hard for me to have to leave. I was confused and didn't know if I could survive until the next day. As I rode the bus back home, I was thinking only of what I could do to get dope. If I tried not getting high until the next day, I might panic in the middle of the night and do something crazy. I thought maybe Nellie might have a few dollars stashed away. She had become an expert in hiding money, but she had gotten too good at it.

I knocked on the door, and Nellie opened it.

"What happened?" she asked at the sight of me. "How come your back?"

I told her, and she could sense how disappointed I was. I sat down without even taking off my coat. I was already feeling sick. Hours had passed since my last shot.

It's strange how that works. It had only been a half hour since I left the church, and I didn't feel sick when I left. It reminded me of the time I went to kick my first habit.

Eventually one learns to recognize the various stages of sickness. When an addict is in a place where he can't get any dope, he gets very sick when he goes into his withdrawal. When he knows that he can get dope, there is a sort of pre-sickness that he feels before the real sickness of withdrawal starts. How that happens I don't know, but it is real.

I had all the symptoms of pre-sickness. My nose was running, and I felt that tickle in my throat that made me nauseous. I kept coughing to keep from throwing up. Nellie knew the signs very well. She was familiar with the various stages of sickness and especially the stage I called the "act" of sickness. She could see that I was not acting and told me not to worry. Then she threw a jacket over her shoulders and said she was going next door for a minute. I thought perhaps she was going to borrow some money, so I was totally surprised when she returned in a few minutes and handed me a bag of dope.

I took it and asked, "How did you get this, Nellie? Did you buy it from someone?"

"No. I thought maybe there would be a time when you might need some, so I saved it from the dope I was holding for you." Then she opened her other hand and showed me another bag, explaining, "This one is for the morning."

She had managed to do that without me realizing it, but showing me that second bag was a mistake. I had been shooting one bag at a time for a few days now, and although it was holding me, I wasn't really getting the high I wanted. I thought of how nice it would be to shoot both bags at the same time to get a real nice high. I convinced her by telling her that since I was leaving in the morning, I wouldn't need the bag for then. It would add up to the same thing.

After a slight protest, she handed me the second bag. I went into the bathroom and shot them both. I felt a good rush from the shot, a feeling that every junkie looks for. After cleaning the works and parting them away. I went into the living room, sat down, and nodded in front of the television set. I didn't realize at the time that this would be the last time in my life that I would do that.

XV

A LONG AND HARD DAY FOLLOWED, BUT eventually I was in a car on my way up to Mountaindale. It was a two-hour ride that was pure agony. They could not get transportation until about eight p.m., and I had been in the church since nine a.m. I hadn't had any dope since the night before, so I was already into the withdrawal. I was a mess by the time I got there.

We pulled up along the driveway, which had led to a very large, three-story building. Some of the rooms on the second and third floor had lights on. The entire first floor was dark.

The five of us got out of the car, and with our bags in hand, started walking towards the front door. As sick as I was, it felt great getting out of that car and being able to stretch my legs. By the time we climbed the stairs, someone inside had turned on the lights on the first floor guess they had heard the car doors being slammed and knew someone had arrived.

The front door opened, and when we entered, about half a dozen residents greeted us. Someone came to take my bags and greeted me with a hug. "Glad to see you brother," he said.

It was obvious these guys were full of joy.

Some of the others started coming down, and I was surprised when I recognized about half of them. Since the church was in my old neighborhood, most of those I knew were from around there. Some of the others were either from jail or the hospitals I had been in.

Everyone was greeting us now. The ones who knew me greeted me by name. Those who didn't know me, greeted me as a brother, but everyone would say. "Praise the lord." this was a real strange experience and completely new to me. There I was, looking at a bunch of ex-dope fiends praising the lord and putting their arms around me. If this were the street, we would all be looking to cut each other's throats for a bag of dope.

The person who had driven us up there stepped forward and asked, "is the director here?"

One of the fellows responded, "No. He's in Pennsylvania trying to get some money for the program."

The driver looked around. "Is anyone planning on making coffee?"

A man near the back of the group spoke up. "The water's already on. Should be just a few more minutes."

Within about a half an hour, we were all sitting with a cup of freshly made coffee in our hands.

The driver drank his coffee. Then he and the other person with him left, leaving us three new brothers behind. It seemed strange to me that out of all the guys who had been at the church the night before, it was just the three of us who had made it to the camp.

I didn't sleep at all that night. The other two guys who had come up with me did go to sleep eventually, but I stayed up to see the sunrise. Out of all the times that I kicked the habits, not being able to sleep was what bothered me the most—that and the pain in my legs.

The next morning, I heard someone moving around and immediately went to see who had gotten up. I was surely ready for some more of that attention I had receives the night before. Maybe someone could get me a nice warm cup of coffee.

I headed for the place where they had received us the night before, but no one was there. The door to the kitchen was closed. I went over, I then walked over to the front entrance and went out onto the porch. I could see someone walking across the road, but he was too far away for me to recognize. I realized then how desperate I was to have someone to talk to.

I didn't go back upstairs. I figured someone would be coming down to cook breakfast. They might even be able to give me a cup of coffee. I didn't know what time it was, but it seemed that someone should be up by now.

As I continued to wait, I noticed how the building was in need of a lot of repair. It must have been a nice place at one time, I thought, but that was a long time ago. Another very noticeable thing was that nothing was locked up. Even in the hospitals we were always locked in, I told myself this was where I was going to be. I was a good hundred miles from the Bronx, and I knew there wasn't any dope nearby that could get.

I now started hearing the movement upstairs. When I got up to the first floor, I could smell the coffee brewing. Someone had a coffee pot in their room and was making coffee. I was like a bloodhound trying to find where the smell was coming from. At last, one of the brothers opened his door and saw me in the hallway.

"How are you feeling?" he asked.

Before I could answer him, he said, "Don't worry. just trust the lord."

The words were reassuring, but at that moment, the smell of coffee had my attention.

"Do you know where I could get a cup of coffee?" I asked. He gave me a knowing smile. "Sure. Just let me find you a cup."

He entered his room and came out with an empty cup in his hand. After giving it to me, he sent me down the hall, sort of pointing to the room.

"Just ask them to give you some," he told me.

I followed his instructions with good results.

An hour passed, and soon the building was humming with activity. It was Saturday and no one had to do any jobs. The place didn't have any structure. Everyone went around doing as they felt, but things appeared to be going smoothly. Some of the brothers would even pray for me when I looked like I was feeling bad. They would always ask me if I felt better after the prayer, and I would say yes. Actually, I didn't feel better physically. What made me feel better was that they cared enough to pray for me. I didn't have the heart to tell them that I still felt sick.

The days went by, and I got better fast. We had bible class in the morning, work in the afternoons, and services at night.

After about five days of being there, I had an experience unlike anything I had ever had before in my life. It happened at one of the evening services. The person who was preaching that night hit me with a lot of guilt. I was certain he was preaching directly at me. The guilt was so strong, at one point I actually broke down and cried; in fact, the feeling was so overwhelming I completely lost control.

The preacher called me up to the front. He also called up a few of the other brother. They all put their hands on me and started to pray out loud. I was still crying, and I could not control myself. It was as though I suddenly realized all the bad things I had done.

They prayed for me for about ten minutes. Finally, I got control of myself and began calming down. One by one they took their hands off me and sat back down. I was still up front when the brother who was preaching asked me how I felt.

"Better," I said.

I actually did feel better. I felt that a tremendous burden had been lifted from my shoulders. The relief was so great that I said the words, "thank you Jesus." over and over, I repeated "thank you, Jesus."

All the brothers started praising the lord. Soon everyone was singing, "oh, how I love Jesus. Oh, how I love Jesus."

I was now jumping up and down, still saying, "thank you, Jesus." I couldn't believe what I was doing but I didn't care. It just felt so good to do it.

After the service ended, a lot of the brothers stayed and talked to me. Some were convinced I had received the Holy Ghost. They said I had to continue to seek the lord, saying that the lord had a job for me to do.

Well, I didn't know what had happened. All I knew was that I felt good. It was the first time I had ever had such an experience. If it felt so good, and this was only the first time; I reasoned that surely it would get even better.

In the months to follow, I grew close to a few people, but Sammy became my closest friend. We knew each other from the streets, and the friendship continued to grow stronger here in the camp. Sammy left after about two months, but he came to visit. I would also see him when I was out on pass.

Nellie did very well while I was in camp. She was on welfare and that, at least, paid the basics. When I came home for weekend visits, she would go to church with me. She wasn't really into the teachings of the church, but she always came with me because she could see how it was helping me. We would take the kids with us. We were doing things together, and that was great.

When I had been at the church several months, the director made plans to leave. Consequently, the church sent up three directors to run the camp: Joe (the ex-addict who preached the first day I came to church), Sammy, and Hector. I had been there for about six months when they informed me, they needed assistance and were depending on me to help them. At that time, I held the position of dean of the house, which meant I was in charge of all the work and setting up the services at night. This was a very responsible job, and gradually the brothers looked to me as a leader. I had a couple of minor problems in the beginning, but now I was actually living the life. I had the respect of all the brothers at the camp.

It was great having three directors. They had more experience than we did, and each night one of them would preach to us. Eventually, though, they started to leave. Joe was first. He was always more of an evangelist than a director. Sammy left next. He was good in the sense that he liked to fix things. He tore down a lot with the hope of rebuilding, but he left before he could finish the job. It was his wife Arlene who directed in the true sense. So that left only Hector. He lived in one of the apartments with his wife and would seldom come out. I was just about the only person in camp who could see him. I ran the entire camp practically alone. A year passed, and I was still in the camp.

I didn't want to be there that long, but I didn't want to leave until I was sure I was strong enough to survive. My friends and family couldn't seem to understand my reasons for staying so long. They probably were thinking that I was trying to avoid my responsibilities to my family, that was bothering me a lot, but I wasn't going to let it destroy what I knew I had to do. I just didn't want to use drugs anymore, and I wanted it that way for the rest of my life.

I had been at camp for about a year when Juan came with his brother Carlos. After a shaky start, Juan got real serious about the Lord. Since they knew a lot about plumbing and electricity, the two were able to help a lot in putting the camp back together. While they were there, we built a new kitchen, chapel, and dining area. Some other brothers who knew carpentry, plastering, and painting also put in a lot of work. Eventually the camp started to look real good.

As time passed, I found myself coming home on days other than weekends. Sometimes I would spend a week at home to check out how I felt. Each time I gained a little more confidence.

The camp taught me a lot about life. It gave me a value system that is still with me today. I remember the good times and the bad. Sometimes we went without food, and sometimes in the winter we went without oil for the furnace, but we would always survive anything that came. Faith, I learned, is a powerful weapon. I also found that because of these experiences I had become a better man.

Nellie became pregnant again and was expecting in March of 1965. I began to look at February as the time to leave camp. I still had some rough edges to work on, but my attitude had changed dramatically, and I felt I would survive.

I sat down with Nellie, and we made plans about how we were going to deal with my returning home. She was very happy over the decision. We were both feeling good knowing the time was finally coming for us to be together. She was still going along with me to church, but she was doing it mostly for me. She had been catholic all her life and had no desire to change. I admired her for never trying to discourage me in what I was doing.

The time arrived for me to leave. I fasted for five days that week. All the brothers chipped in and bought me a bible as a gift. (I still have that bible and whenever I look at it, it brings me the memory of the camp.) When I got home, I got a job in a car wash, mostly to get some money fast. I got involved with the church with the same energy that I had at the camp, and now attended just about every night. Nellie and the kids went with me most the time. I also joined the choir and was working with the children of the church.

Leslie Lynn was born on March 2, 1965. Our first daughter. After three boys, we finally had a daughter. Her time was just right. She didn't have to go through what the other children had gone through, especially Mikey, our oldest. He could remember the hard times, times that would leave a lasting impression in his life.

In the Pentecostal religion, one has to make some very hard sacrifices, some of which I made out of fear more than anything else. It was often very difficult to follow the doctrine because I had to give up so much. My fear was that if I didn't follow what I was taught, I would end up using drugs again. I was confused. I knew that I had stopped using drugs. While in the camp it was much easier to follow Christ, but out in the real world it was not as easy. Using or not using drugs was not the problem, it was the other things, like not going to the movies or parties, and having to treat my wife and children as sinners if they didn't follow me in the church or going to the beach wearing bathing suits. I could go on and on about what I had to give up. I was really struggling with all this for a while.

On the other hand, I did not want these things to lead me back to using drugs. I didn't have the desire to use drugs; I was afraid that if I did these things, I would be ungrateful and fall out of the grace of God. I was being torn between two worlds, and I didn't know what was going to happen.

The only person who knew what I was going through was Nellie. I didn't dare talk about it with anyone, not even her, but she seemed to know. I think she had gotten more involved with the church because she thought it might help me. She even stopped wearing makeup and we started going to church more often. In an indirect way, I must have let her know that she had to do that.

After about three months of battling with this, I found a temporary solution. In one of the services mama Leo made a plea for someone to go to the camp to help Hector. It presented a perfect solution for me. It seemed strange that things were so hard for me, and I decided that it must be that I was too weak. I didn't want anyone to know how weak I was. It was too hard to just come out and say that I wanted to go back to the camp, but volunteering to go back to help was perfect. So, I volunteered.

Nellie was not too happy with that decision, and she let me know it. Even some of the brothers who were going to church with me could not understand why I would do something like that. I started to have second thoughts about it myself, but I did it anyway.

Once again, I became involved with the operation of the camp. I still came home on occasion, and sometimes Nellie and the kids would come up to the camp and stay with me. This went on for another year, and once more I was feeling strong enough to leave.

Some of the brothers who left the camp would not always return to New York City. One of the places where they went was New Haven, Connecticut, the location of one of the churches that supported the camp. Consequently, those who went there would make trips to the camp about twice a year. I had gotten to be good friends with the pastor of the church at New Haven.

He would bring his whole congregation to the camp. It was always a joyous event when we knew they were coming, because they brought carloads of food and other needs.

A few of the members of that church were from the Bronx, and I spoke with them. I was curious to know why they had moved to New Haven. They told me that life was easier out there, and that there were plenty of jobs. It was enough to start me thinking about going out there myself. The brothers from camp all appeared to be doing well in New Haven. They all found a place to live and got jobs. It was then that I started talking to Nellie about moving out there.

Nellie was not too thrilled about moving, because she didn't know anyone there at all. All her family and friends were in the Bronx. I told her I would go first and check it out. If I didn't like it, I would come back, and we would forget the whole thing. Although she wasn't very excited about it, she agreed.

When the time came for me to leave the camp for the second time, I was thinking a lot more about my commitment to the Lord. My plans now had a purpose. I would attempt to start a new life in New Haven, find a job and a place to move my family. I would then dedicate my life to helping the addicts find Christ.

XVI

IT WAS MAY 2, 1966. I had just turned thirty-one years old the day before and was once again leaving Nellie to search for my sanity. This time, however, there were four children left behind. I had not used drugs for two and a half years, but I still had not found that I was free. I had the Lord in my heart now, but I still didn't have the peace that was supposed to come with it. I was going to a different place, and I didn't know what was going to happen.

Maybe things will not work out, I told myself. And I can find the peace I've never had except for my stay at camp. Or I could be on my way back in a week or a month, But I will try. I have to conquer being able to live in the real world.

It was a beautiful day when I took the train to New Haven. I was rather surprised that the ride was so short. I'd taken subway rides in New York that took longer. When the train pulled into New Haven, I called the Reverend, and he came to pick me up. It was the middle of the afternoon, so he took me to his house. He lived with his family above the storefront church that he was the pastor of. The building must have been some kind of office at one time, because the apartment was shaped funny.

We entered into a very large room that reminded me of a waiting room. It had what must have been a lot of private offices on one side. They were now being used as bedrooms. In the rear was the kitchen that appeared to have been added recently. The Reverend's wife gave me a warm greeting and prepared coffee for me. A few of the church members dropped in while I was there, talked awhile, and then left.

I was waiting for one of the brothers who were at the camp to come and pick me up. They knew I was coming and had offered to come and get me after they got off work. I waited impatiently. I felt uncomfortable, because all this was new to me.

The brothers who had come to New Haven before me were Juan, Ray, and Walter. Walter was the first to arrive. He had gotten an apartment, and Juan and Ray were living with him. They were all working and going to church. From what I was told by the Reverend and his wife, they were all doing quite well. I was going to stay with them. Juan was going to talk to his boss about a job for me. If everything worked out the way I hoped, I would be together with my family soon.

I hadn't seen much of New Haven at that point, only what I could see between the train station and the Reverend's house. It was different from the Bronx. I hoped it would be right. One of the things that Nellie and I had talked about was that it would be good to get the children out of New York. Things were so bad for us in New York; we were starting to be afraid for the kids. It just had to be better here.

Ray was the first to arrive at the Reverend's house. I was so glad to see an old friend. We greeted each other with a hug and talked for a little while. About a half hour later Walter came in, and it was the same thing.

They took me over to the apartment and then Juan joined us. It was a joyful reunion, and I was starting to feel really good about the decision to come to New Haven. I must have asked hundreds of questions about the church and its members, their jobs, and so on.

I think they were getting tired of all the questions because eventually they said, "Don't worry, just take it easy, and everything will be all right."

Juan had spoken to his boss, and his boss wanted him to bring me in for an interview. I went with him the next morning and was hired. I had not worked in over three years, except for a few weeks at the car wash. I was just glad that he didn't ask me about that. I was sure he wouldn't hire me if he knew I had been an addict.

When I told him I knew a lot about tool and die making, he took me upstairs and introduced me to Frank, the foreman of the tool and die making department. He wanted to see if I could do the work. After about two weeks of working with him, he decided he wanted to keep me. I liked the job and the other workers. I started at a dollar and sixty cents per hour, which was minimum salary at the time, but when Frank saw that I knew what I was doing, he put me in for a good raise.

I went back to the Bronx to see Nellie and the kids every chance I got. She had been complaining of some pains in the stomach. Though they were not continuous, when they struck, they almost drove her crazy. She had been getting them even before I went to Connecticut, but we hadn't done anything about it.

When she went to the hospital, they couldn't find out the cause I didn't know how serious it was until she got them on one of the weekends that I was home. The pain was so strong she threw herself to the floor in agony. The only things that made her feel better were some strong drugs the doctor in the hospital had prescribed. I took her back to the hospital, but still, they could not find the trouble. This time they gave her an appointment to go to the clinic so they could look further into the problem.

After we got home from the hospital, Nellie took her medication and fell asleep. We had been up practically all night. I woke her when I was ready to leave. I said I would call her during the week to see how she was, but if she felt sick, she should call me at the Reverend's house and I would take the train down.

After she went to get checked out in the clinic, they were finally able to determine the cause of the pains; she had developed stones in her gallbladder. It was recommended that she have an operation to have them removed as soon as possible. It was not good news, but I think we were both relieved that it wasn't something more serious. I knew that I had imagined all sorts of things. I told her I thought she should go through with the operation as they had suggested. To my surprise she agreed without any hesitation. She probably thought of those attacks and didn't want to go through it anymore.

I stayed with the kids and Nellie had the operation. She recovered very quickly. The last couple of days she was in the hospital, her mother stayed with the kids, and I returned to work.

For the first three months I was in New Haven, everything went along better than I would ever have imagined. I saved every penny I could. I attended all the church services except for those on the weekends; that time was spent with Nellie and the kids. I even started to take driving lessons. I was thirty-one years old and had never had a car or a driver's license. I actually felt as if I had reached a milestone in my life when I took my driving test and passed. Now I had more than the man with the paper bag lunch.

I bought an old jalopy for a hundred and twenty-five dollars. It was much easier going to see Nellie now that I could drive. Everyone was so excited when I drove the car into the city. My son Mikey, who was up the street visiting my mother at the time, saw me driving up the street and made fun of my jalopy.

"Well, son," I told him, putting my arm around his shoulder, "maybe it doesn't look like much, but it runs well."

It was the first car I ever owned, so to me it was like having a brand new El Dorado, even if no one else thought so.

In September of the same year, I moved the family to Connecticut. I was able to find a four-room apartment on Frank Street. The place was a mess and the landlord let me have it for fifty dollars a month if I agreed to fix it up myself. My father-in-law was a professional painter, and he came up from the Bronx and painted it for us. The place looked a lot better after he finished it, but I don't think anything we could have done would have made it really nice.

We lived there for a little over a year and had to move under an emergency situation. The redevelopment agency purchased the building and planned to tear it down so they could use the lot for a schoolyard. That was fine with me. Right away the agency set about finding us another apartment. It was a six-family house, and four families had already been relocated.

On one very cold night, the plumbing in the empty apartments froze and broke. As a result, no water was coming up to our apartment. After that happened it was amazing how fast an apartment was found for us.

The apartment we moved to was actually worse than the one we had left, but it was warm, and at that moment, that was all that mattered. This place was also going to be part of the same schoolyard. We lived in this apartment for a year, and the redevelopment agency still hadn't found us a permanent place.

Almost three years went by since I first came to Connecticut. In that time I kept very busy. Juan and I were always involved with bringing any addicts we found to programs in New York. Sometimes we would pick up other addicts in New York and bring them to New Haven.

Occasionally we would get groups together and drive to Mountaindale and visit the camp.

It was on one of those visits that I found Carlos at the camp. (You might remember Carlos from way back in my dealing days. He was the one who was partners with Munge.) I never imagined that Carlos would get religion, but there he was. Not only was he at camp, he was the Dean of the program.

After talking for a while, we began reminiscing about the old days. Carlos and I had done a little time together in the Bronx County Jail. (If I remember correctly, I got out on bail in about a week, and Carlos went to Sing Sing Prison.) Carlos, Munge, and I had once pulled a burglary in a grocery store. We stole all the cigarettes and sold them to buy dope.

Carlos was quite skinny at the time, and he was the only one who could squeeze through the opening we had made in the store.

Later Carlos left Mountaindale and eventually started using drugs again. One day his mother called me and I went down to his house in the Bronx to try to convince him to come to New Haven. I was not able to get a hold of him the first time, but I got him on the second trip. He had been using drugs for a few months and was pretty well hooked by then.

When I arrived at his house, he was packed and ready to go, so I took him to Juan's apartment. Since Juan already had a few ex-addicts living with him, we threw a mattress in the corner of the kitchen, and it was there that Carlos kicked his habit completely, he was working and going to church. Together we became quite active in trying to work with the addicts. We tried to start a program ourselves but failed. We would sometimes get discouraged and thought it was hopeless, but then we would start again.

A lot of addicts came and went. Some did well and some did bad, but we kept working and doing the best we could.

It was about this time that I met Doug. He was a social worker with the welfare department in New Haven. He used to come to the church, and since he spoke no Spanish, I would interpret for him. He was older than we were, but he became interested in the work we were doing. He became an ex-addict by adoption and went everywhere with us. Now the core of the group was up to four. Still others came and went.

Many of the ex-addicts who had gotten themselves together stayed with the group but moved on to different places. They remained clean and off drugs. Two such individuals were George and Nelson. They were around long enough to contribute in our goal of starting a program, the Christian Ex-addicts Association. We collected dues and used the money to help the programs that we visited. We also sent money to Mama Leo to help her with the camp.

While I was involved with all these outside activities, I still went to church, taught Sunday school, went to Bible seminary two nights a week, and was in charge of working with the children of the church, Even though I was very busy with the church and the drug rehabilitation program, I still worked for the same company and had even gotten a promotion to foreman in the production department.

In 1968 we moved to a house that we bought a year later. My children were going to school, and we were starting to have some problems with Mikey. I wasn't sure, but maybe it was that he was starting to have problems with us. Mikey was sixteen years old at the time, and for about the past two years he seemed to be building up quite a bit of resentment. He reminded me so much of myself when I was his age.

Apparently, I had put so much pressure on him to go to church that it made me blind to Mikey's needs. He mostly hung around with kids who seemed to be having the same feelings he had. When he started to outwardly rebel, I started to put even more pressure on him. It was like adding wood to a fire that you want to put out. He lost interest in school and finally stopped going completely. Not aware of what we were doing, Nellie and I continued to put pressure on him. He dealt with it by agreeing to join the navy. I guess he figured we were not going to accept his leaving school very easily.

Joining the navy was an opportunity for Mikey to get away from the pressure, so he took it. He enlisted for four years. It was painful for Nellie and me knowing he felt he had to get away from us, because there was a lot of love between us. There was never any doubt that he loved us and that we loved him. I think that was the main reason why he did it the he did. Nevertheless, it really shook my faith.

Although Robert way was very different from Mikey, he was starting to show the same resentment. He showed it a different way. He didn't hang out with any gangs but went mostly to where he could dance. He had learned to do that well. He liked Latin music and always wanted to play the trumpet. I think it was because of that that he didn't like to hang out with gangs.

Robert's way of handling his anger was to run away from home. He ran away for three days when he was about fifteen years old, and Nellic and I almost went crazy. I went out ever day looking for him. I didn't want to have the same thing happen to him that had happened to me. When he came back, we sat down with him and talked about it. He was much easier going than Mikey, so things worked out without as much complication. We were able to get him a trumpet, and he started to take lessons.

By now I had gotten to the point where I couldn't sit in the congregation of the church and listen to anyone tell me how to raise my children. It was up to Nellie and me to raise them the way we saw fit. Whatever happened was going to be solely our responsibility. I wouldn't put that on anyone else. For whatever reason, raising our children in the Christian way wasn't going to do it for us. I had to learn to be more flexible in my understanding of parenthood. Even Nellie used to tell me that. We loved our children and wanted the best for them. That's the way most parents are, but we put too much pressure on the boys to do things our way.

Fortunately, Stevie and Leslie did not reach that awkward age before we discovered this.

XVII

FOUR YEARS HAD GONE BY SINCE we came to New Haven. It was an action-packed four years from 1966 to 1970, but it was a great four years for Nellie and I. I say great, not because we didn't have any problems, but because I didn't use drugs. Not only did I not use drugs, but I didn't drink either. With all that happened (and it was plenty), I had survived through it all, even though the riots in New Haven. The riots were a horror that I won't touch on now, except to say that it made me realize that nothing was more important than my family.

Just before going into 1970, two important things happened: we stopped going to church completely, and I changed jobs. The company I worked for went out of business. I then got a job as a housing inspector with the redevelopment agency in New Haven. Carlos helped me get that job. He had been working with the agency himself for about a year at the time, but his job was at the family relocation office on the other side of town.

I made a lot more money when I worked in the factory, but this job was good. I had never worked in a place where I didn't get my hands dirty before and found the job to be very easy and sometimes boring.

About the same time, Nellie got a job as a dental assistant at Hill Health Center. Even though I was bringing home less money, now with both of us working, we weren't having any trouble making ends meet.

Before Mikey had left for the navy, he was getting interested in playing the congas. Since he knew I played in bands when I was younger, he asked me to teach him some beats. For the short time before he went to boot camp, I began teaching him. When he left, I continued to practice. Since I was no longer going to church or meeting much with the ex-addicts, I had to put my energy into something. I would come from work and go down to the basement and practice every day.

I missed the guys from church. I also missed the meetings. It appeared that my dream of getting a program for addicts was never going to happen. That was what hurt me most. I didn't feel guilty for having left the church; what really bothered me was the program. I always felt it was no accident that I came to New Haven. I really felt that I had failed. It was the most important thing in my life, and I hadn't been able to stay with it long enough to see it happen.

With all the turmoil I was going through, I never thought of using drugs or drinking. I never actually drank in the past, so that was never a problem. The one thing I did do was start smoking again. I hadn't smoked cigarettes for years, but now I started smoking again.

Things went like that for about six months. Then one of the guys called me and told me that the guys wanted to meet with me. That night they came over to the house, and we all sat around in the living room. They had come because they were concerned about me. They did everything they could to try to convince me to return to church. I had suspected they would come. I remembered how many times I had done what they were doing. I was ready with all the answers. I didn't want to be so convincing so as to cause anyone of them to follow me. And I still wanted to be part of the group so I could be involved with the plans of opening the drug program. But I couldn't do it that way.

Finally, they realized that I was not going to be convinced. We continued to talk about what they had been doing, and they said they hadn't been doing much. No one was about to give enough money to get the program going. Everyone thought we were doing a great thing, but the money wasn't coming in. They seemed to want me to get involved, even though I wasn't going to church.

It felt really good to talk about the program with the guys. In all the months that I was not involved, I had thought about a lot of things that we could try. I began to share with the guys and they seemed to like my ideas.

We continued talking, and I didn't realize how late it was getting. Everyone had been so involved that the time had flown by quickly. Before they left, I wanted to find out what their next step was going to be. Was I merely going to share my ideas with them at this one meeting, or would they allow me to be part of the group again? I waited.

While they were setting the date for the next meeting, I just sat and glanced around the room. Juan was sitting at my left, then Doug, Carlos, Indio and at my right was George. They agreed on a day.

Juan looked at me and said, "Is that a good day for you?"

When he said that, I think my heart skipped a few beats. I tried to be as casual as I could, but the excitement was just too much for me.

I got up from my chair and said, "Yes, that day is just fine."

We ended the meeting hugging each other.

"This time we go all the way," I heard Carlos say from across the room.

Someone else agreed by saying that nothing was going to stop us now. It was a meeting of rededication.

After they left, I found it hard going to sleep. I guessed it was all the excitement from the meeting. I was thinking of what was going to happen when we met again.

The next morning, I told Nellie about the meeting since she had gone to sleep before we were finished. She also got very excited over what had happened.

At last, the day of the next meeting finally arrived. It was held at Doug's house in Hamden, Connecticut. The first problem we addressed was why we were not getting any church or agency to fund the program. We remembered that someone had once told us that no one in their right mind was going to give five ex-drug addicts that kind of money. We decided to get a board of directors together. We would find reputable committee people. We prepared a long list of people and divided the list among ourselves. During the week each of us met with the various people. Some couldn't accept because of prior commitments, but others were happy to join our cause.

At the next meeting we formed the first board of directors. Father Joe, a Catholic priest, was elected chairman of the board. I was elected vice chairman. As we continued meet, we added other people. We needed a board that would be as committed as we were. It appeared that we had what we needed.

Our primary concern was to serve the Hispanic addicts in our area. That was what we wanted to do all along.

When we first started, we wanted to run the program like the Christian Youth Crusade, but we couldn't get the churches to support it. Now we were using a different approach. If we wanted to get the state and government to give us funds, we had to take the religious concept out. We decided to use the therapeutic community approach. We prepared a set of by-laws and got ourselves incorporated in the later part of 1971. We decided to call the program Crossroads, Inc., a name I had always had in the back of my mind. When I presented it to the board, it was voted on and accepted.

In 1972 we still had no money, but we kept at it. This time we were persistent. We followed each lead until every possibility had been looked into. Then we would move on to something else.

On a few occasions I visited with Dr. Herbert, the Executive Director of the Drug Dependant unit of the Connecticut mental Health Center. I had known him for a few years and was currently serving with him on the Mayor's Drug Task Force. I had a lot of respect for Dr. Herbert, mainly because of his sincerity. I knew he had done a lot to bring treatment programs into New Haven, even though I couldn't remember him getting the recognition he deserved. He had always been supportive of Crossroads, and I knew I could count on him whenever I wanted his help. He had even written some letters of support for us in the past when we needed them.

One day in mid-1973, I was working in my office and got a call from Dr. Herbert. He told me he had received a call from Hartford informing him that Crossroads was going to receive funds to open the program. I could not believe my ears. I asked him to repeat what he had just said. I had to hear him say it again. The reason they had called him first was that they wanted to know if he would give us technical assistance. He told them he would. I guess he couldn't resist the temptation to call me and let me know.

After I hung up the phone, I just sat there, bewildered. I was alone in the office that I shared with two other housing inspectors, and suddenly, with my hand still on the phone, I could no longer hold back my emotions. Impulsively, I started to cry. After a couple of minutes, I pulled myself together and started calling everyone who had been involved with Crossroads. When I got home, I shared my joy with Nellie, and she was equally thrilled with the news. She knew how hard we had worked for the program and what it meant to me.

It was just about that time that I was offered a chance to play congas in one of the local bands. Freddie, the leader of the band had heard from a friend of Mikey's that I could play them.

I accepted the position and really enjoyed playing on weekends. A lot of the musicians were heavy drinkers, but I didn't drink at all. It had been ten years since I had stopped using drugs, and in those ten years I hadn't used any alcohol either. It was rare that I ever thought of getting high on drugs. As far as drinking was concerned, I thought of that even less. I wasn't around people who did much drinking, so it was easy to forget about it; however, all that was about to change.

I always had a great love for music; even while I was in church, I liked to sing a lot. Now I was playing in a band. We would play for nightclubs, weddings, and other events. I would see the other members of the band drinking at all these events. The saxophone player even carried a bottle in his sax case. Besides seeing them drink while on the job, I was also exposed during the trip to work. I would drive my own car to the clubs. Since I wasn't familiar with the locations of the nightclubs, I would follow one of the other cars. They would usually stop at a liquor store to get some liquor.

I had a station wagon at the time, and I helped out by transporting the amplifiers and speakers. I would also give other musicians rides to the jobs. Even the guys riding with me would want to stop and pick up something. Once we hit the highway, the bottles started being passed around. Although I didn't say anything, I wasn't crazy about it. I was new in the band and didn't know how they would take it if I told them not to drink in the car. It was just a matter of routine with them. Maybe I was the odd ball.

Once there. I was continually being offered drinks at the clubs. I didn't accept them at first, but eventually I would accept a couple in the course of the night. I did this because when I refused; I always felt that I was offending the person who was buying me the drink. In all the years that I was using drugs, I had never really got into drinking. I wasn't aware of the unwritten rules. Naturally I didn't drink while I was in church, so here I was, thirty-seven years old and not knowing that when someone buys you a drink, you have to buy them one back.

It didn't take long for me to start looking forward to going out as play. I think I was starting to like the drinking more than the playing I had enough control to drink only at the dances. I didn't think it was very cool to be drinking in the car. I had a low image of people who did that.

In December of the same year, Crossroads got the money in needed and opened. Some of the board members convinced me to take the director's job. I really wanted the job so it didn't take much convincing In early 1974 we accepted the first four Hispanic residents.

At the time, a fellow by the name of Kevin worked for Dr. Herbert and was sort of on loan to us as a consultant. He was a great help to us. We were new at this, and his input helped us through this difficult time.

Genny and I were the first people hired. We hired the rest of the staff. Rolando was a graduate from Daytop. He had the experience of how to run a therapeutic committee. William was another counselor hired, but he left for Florida after about a year. Juan became another counselor. When William left, we hired Joe. Joe had also been a graduate of Daytop and had a lot of experience on how it worked. He was very likeable, but we eventually realized he was an alcoholic. This really caused a lot of conflict with the staff and the board of directors. I tried to help him as much as I could, but it was hopeless. I found myself becoming his counselor, and that stood in the way of my job as director. Eventually Joe did something outrageous, and I had to let him go.

After a couple of close calls, we were able to survive that first year, I continued to play with Freddie on the weekends. My drinking had progressed very little. I saw myself drinking like everyone else. I still drank only at the dances and at social events. I even kept liquor in the house, and the bottles would collect dust on them. When I played on the weekends and drank, I never wanted to pick up a drink the next day.

At the same time, my youngest son Stevie was starting to learn how to play the trombone. I was able to get him a trombone from a cousin of mine, uncle Willie's son, who was a bandleader. This man was hard to get hold of, so I kept calling his mother until she got the trombone for me. Willie and she had gotten a divorce, and Willie was doing time in prison again. Although they had gotten a divorce, Nellie remained good friends with her, and we would occasionally go down to visit her.

I was playing congas, Robert was starting to sound good on the trumpet, and Steve was starting on the trombone. Mikey had about a year to go before getting out of the navy. He had lost interest in the congas and was now getting into the timbales. (You know what's coming, don't you?)

While he was still in the service, Mikey decided to get married. He had met Yvonne in Meriden and had fallen in love. They had a very nice wedding, and after a short stay in Connecticut, Mikey went back to finish his time in the navy. Their son was born in July of 1973. Mikey completed his four years in the navy in 1974 and moved back to New Haven.

I finished the attic for him and Yvonne. Nellie and I were grandparents now, and Nellie was crazy about her grandchild. She was always buying things for him. (She's still that way with all our grandchildren.)

The program was doing well. We were able to attract additional funding to increase staff. Ana came to work in 1975. I had worked with her at the redevelopment agency. She came to Crossroads as a volunteer. She and Nellie would raise money and food every Christmas for the residents' Christmas party. They always made it possible for the residents to have a nice dinner and get gifts every Christmas. That Christmas I invited Freddie and the band to come in and play for the residents. As usual, I had his cooperation.

By now my sons had served their apprenticeship with Freddie's band. First it was Robert, and the others followed. We would often talk about starting our own band. In the two succeeding years, we talked about it more and more. It even got to the point where we would invite some musicians to my house and rehearse.

Finally, we broke from Freddie and started out on our own. It was a lot of hard work putting everything together. After a couple of months of rehearsing, we were ready to start playing in clubs. The band sounded great, and we were able to get a lot of work. We started doing a lot of jobs in New York. The clubs that we played in would always invite us back. We still had a lot to learn, but we were steadily improving.

I was getting heavier in my drinking, and I was now doing things that I wouldn't have done before. At first, I would stop to buy a half-pint bottle on my way to the dance. After a night of playing until early morning, I would drive home under the influence. Nellie started to notice that I was drinking more than before. She brought it to my mind, but I didn't pay her much mind. I only drank when I played, so how could she tell me that I was drinking too much? I would be able to rest up on Sundays and go to work on Monday. In spite of whatever I told her, she kept telling me that I was drinking too much. The progression was so slow that I could easily make myself believe I had control of it. But down inside I was getting the feeling that something was wrong--and I wasn't trying to stop. I liked what I was doing. And I wasn't going to let anyone interfere with that.

As I see it now, I already had the alcoholic mentality. Let's look at the first step one takes in joining Alcoholics Anonymous: "We admitted we were powerless over alcohol, that our lives had become unmanageable." I wasn't powerless over alcohol every day; I was powerless only on weekends. Powerless for two reasons: one that I had to drink every weekend, and two, that I couldn't control the amount I drank. I was well past just having a few social drinks.

I can now see a lot of things that I didn't want to see then. Back then I didn't want to think much about it. Anytime I found myself thinking that I was having a problem, I would convince myself that I didn't by using comparisons. After I justified myself, I would stop thinking about it. It was like trying to balance the scale with an imaginary weight.

XVIII

THE PROGRAM WAS MY SALVATION. IT was what would always pull me back to the world. When I got in on Monday morning, I would think about how I wasn't going to drink the coming weekend. Sometimes I was more successful than other times. But being successful meant only that I drank less.

In 1977 Crossroads opened a house for women. It was the first such program in the state. The women would be allowed to have their children with them while in treatment. We were in the process of hiring staff for the women's house. It offered all the excitement we had when we opened the men's house.

Early in 1977, I decided to call my uncle. My intention was to see if I could get in contact with his son because I wanted to talk to him about something to do with the band. I found out

Willie was in jail again. Apparently, he had a fight with the woman he was living with, and it ended up a big mess. She gave me the telephone number of the jail he was in, and the next day I called. He told me what had happened, and I offered to go down to see him.

It was a three and a half hour drive out to Washington, New Jersey. After driving around the town for about another half hour, I finally found the jail he was in. He was kind of uptight with the whole situation out there. I was surprised that things were not going well for him at that time. The last I had heard he was working in City College in New York as a counselor to the students. Before that he had helped put a program together. I knew he was living in New Jersey, but I didn't realize it was this far away.

After exchanging the routine information, we started to get to the heart of the problem. He was doing a lot of drinking and had lost control of his life. He wasn't using drugs, so I considered that a plus. The important thing was that he was ready for a change. I mentioned Connecticut to him. He seemed to think it was a good idea, but he didn't exactly start jumping for joy; after all, he did have his daughter there with him. We ended the visit on that note, and I headed back to New Haven.

While Willie was in jail, we continued writing back and forth. He kept me informed about what was happening with his case. When I realized that things were starting to look bad for him, I went to see him again. This time I took Ana with me. We were going to try to get him stipulated to Crossroads; I knew it would be better to have a counselor do the work. After all, I was his nephew, and I didn't know how the judge would view that.

Everything worked out for us, and in May of 1977, Willie came to the program. It was rather difficult for him at first because of our relationship, but we both dealt with that, and eventually it all worked out fine.

We had our hands full with hiring staff for the women's house. First, we hired an administrative assistant to help Genny in the business office. Edith had just graduated from Yale and was hired for the position. The director of the women's house had already been hired and was working in the men's house until the women's program started accepting women. Grace was hired for childcare. (I mention them because they are still working at Crossroads and have advanced to higher positions in the program. They have been instrumental in making the women's housework.) The program eventually got away from the hard concept and was doing an outstanding job in helping the residents put their lives together.

My drinking only took place on weekends--except for an occasional Monday—and no one really knew what was happening. I always had the excuse that I went to bed late because I was playing in New York or somewhere. Maybe some people were aware, but they never said anything about it.

I think that turning point was somewhere in 1978. I remember that I was losing control of the band. It even started to show up in some of the playing dates we had. It now had become more important to drink than to have a good band. Since I drank a lot myself, I couldn't say much to the other members of the band when they drank. We disagreed on everything. My son Stevie got so upset at one of the rehearsals that he quit the band. He was mainly upset about something that had happened on the last playing date. (Although he wouldn't say it, I'm sure that it had to do with all the drinking that was going on.)

It was incredible how I managed to keep the band going under all that madness. I remember once firing a singer in the middle of a dance because he didn't remember the words to a song, I wanted him to sing. How I managed to play the congas, I will never know. It must have been done as a boxer fights, purely by instinct. Although knocked out on his feet, he could still swing his arms and move his feet. The only thing left for him was to lie down on the canvas and be counted out.

The band lasted another year, and finally under a heated argument at a nightclub, I announced to all the members that I was going to break up the band. I was sorry the moment I said it, but it was the only thing I could do. Because of my drinking, I was no longer able to manage the band.

Although I was no longer playing, I was still drinking on the weekends. I spent two days drinking and five days thinking about it. I always wanted to learn how to play piano, so I started taking lessons in 1980. I thought it might help me if I got interested in something to occupy my time. Actually, it did for a while. It took me only a year or a little over a year before I was playing piano with a small local band. Although I made a lot of mistakes at first, I kept practicing the numbers until I got them right. The leader of the band was very patient with me, and that helped.

At first, I would be very careful not to drink too much when I went out to play. Getting drunk along with not knowing the numbers too well was a bad combination. But slowly I got better at both.

On one occasion I arrived late at a club where we were to play. When I walked in, the band was already on the stage playing. The leader of the band saw me and gave me a signal to go up and play. The reason I had gotten to the place late was that I had to go to a dinner that was giving awards to outstanding leaders in the community. I was one of the awardees, so I had to go to the dinner. While socializing at the dinner, I had a few drinks. By the time I was called up to receive my award, was already feeling the effects of drinks I had consumed. I had to be careful not to stumble. I headed up to the front and saw nothing but legs, tables, and chairs in my path. It was a real challenge to complete this obstacle course, but I was successful. I thought I deserved an award for being able to go up and get it in the condition I was in.

As I returned to my table, I announced that I had to leave. On my way out I went to the bar and had a quick one for the road.

So now with my piano in one hand and my amplifier in the other hand, I was headed to the back of the stage to set up and join the band on stage. I had a small folding table that I always put my piano on. After opening and setting the piano on top of it, I checked the stage to see where I could put the piano. I saw a spot, and with my hands trying to balance the piano and table, I headed for it.

Needless to say, I didn't have the luck that I had at the awards dinner. The piano went flying in one direction and the table and I went in the other direction. The leader of the band looked at me and shook his head. The people who were dancing stopped to look at me. I looked at the bandleader and started to laugh because I didn't know what else to do. I glanced over to see how my piano was, and from where I sat, it appeared to be okay.

I left everything alone until the band finished the first set. At the end of the set, saw the leader walking toward me, and I started complaining about all the wires that were on the floor. I was blaming the wires for what happened, but I knew different--and so did he. I was able to get away with things like that because there was a lot of drinking going on with the other band members. Not to say they were as bad as I was; I didn't know how they viewed their drinking.

I knew I had a problem, but I was not an alcoholic. How could I be? An alcoholic could not do what I could do. I could stay sober for days at a time. I could go to work every day. I never drank while I was working or ever hid a bottle in my desk drawer. Those were things that alcoholics did. I just liked to drink on weekends, and occasionally I drank too much.

Nellie was not making things easy for me. She stayed on my case constantly. I just couldn't come home on Friday with my bottle of Don Q Puerto Rican Rum anymore. I didn't want her to raise hell about it, so I figured if I bought a smaller bottle, I could sneak it in the house without her noticing. It didn't work for long. After I drank myself to sleep, she would find the bottle and get rid of it somehow. At first it threw me because I couldn't remember if I had actually finished it or not, but I couldn't just ask her about it. She definitely was not going to let me drink in peace. The only time I could do that was when I went out and played with the band. When I wanted to drink on the nights that I wasn't playing, I would have to continuously find new ways to do it.

Nellie was always after me.

"Miguel," she would say, "why don't you try to get help with your problem?"

My answer was always the same: "I don't need any help. I can stop drinking anytime I want to. A lot of people drink the way I do, and I didn't think they're alcoholics."

I guess I wasn't very convincing because she still told me to get some help. It wasn't that I don't realize I had a problem; it was that I didn't want to do anything about it.

I remember the time we were planning our thirtieth wedding anniversary. We had invited a lot of people over, mainly family and friends from New York and my co-workers from Crossroads. I told myself that I wasn't going to do much drinking. Even Nellie told me to try to control myself. I promised myself and knew that I would. It was shaky at best.

There were times I could control myself, but most of the time I couldn't. Well, this was one of the times that I couldn't.

I started drinking early. Although I was mindful of the arrival of most of the guest, it wasn't long before I blacked out. The party was going strong, and I was zonked out in my bedroom.

It must have been around two a.m. when I got up. I felt terrible for having left all the guests. There were only a few people left. They were still there because they were going to stay over. We had the party in the backyard, so I went out looking for something to drink. We had set up a bar in the garage, so that's where I went. I couldn't believe it when I saw that all the liquor was gone. I went back inside, and in between talking to people who were there, I kept looking for something to drink. I could sense that something was happening because Nellie didn't say a word. Finally, I couldn't hold back anymore so I asked if the guests had finished all the liquor.

I think everyone was waiting for that because about five people answered at the same time: "All the liquor is gone."

The next day we watched the videotapes of the party. When I saw myself on the tape, I seemed to be all right up until the time I disappeared. After that I got real nervous because I didn't know what to expect. Someone had videotaped me while I was knocked out in my bed. I felt relieved when the video ended. At least I didn't do anything crazy. I had gotten through it without doing something embarrassing.

XIX

OFTEN TRIED TO FIGURE OUT WHY I could not stop drinking. Why, when I would promise myself to stop on Monday, would I drink again on Friday? It was as if I had an uncontrollable impulse. I tried not to drink on weekends, but I always did. I knew if I didn't stop, I was eventually going to lose everything I had. As much as I feared that the people, I worked with would find out, I still drank.

When Friday came around, I would say, "The hell with it. I'll drink this weekend, and I'll worry about it on Monday" That's how I dealt with my drinking when everything became complicated.

Nellie had gotten to the point where she didn't want to go out with me to any place that served drinks. She never knew when I was going to get into my act. That bothered me a lot, but I knew she was right. I had embarrassed her on a number of occasions. I was even embarrassing my children. I don't think they knew how painful it was for me to put them through the things I put them through.

Although I hadn't reached depths that I had during my heroin addiction, I did feel that way sometimes. I had lost control, and I didn't like myself for it. I put on a good act for most people, but I knew what was becoming of me. I wanted help, but I didn't know how to get it. I had to try to do this on my own.

Being the director of a drug treatment program helped me from going over the edge completely, but it also stood in my way. I had a lot of respect in the field, and I thought I would lose that respect if they found out. That would have been very hard for me to deal with.

I knew this could not continue. It would come out sooner or later. If I could just stop drinking, everything would just fall back into place for me.

Different thoughts came to me at different times. Most of the time I would think about stopping my drinking, but there were times when I thought about disappearing for a week and just staying drunk. Thank God I never did.

The more that time went by, the more serious the crisis became. I was heading for destruction, and I didn't know how to stop it. It wasn't that I wanted to self-destruct; destruction was the result. Like jumping out of a plane and my parachute not opening. How could I deal with the impact of hitting the earth?

On October 11, 1984, my daughter Leslie was returning home from a trip she took that had to do with the army reserve. She had been away for about two weeks, and I was to go to LaGuardia Airport to pick her up. It was a Thursday, and I had to leave about an hour early from my job to be there on time to meet her plane.

That morning when I spoke with Nellie about the trip, I had no idea of the nightmare I was going to encounter. I'm sure that Nellie wasn't worried about any problems either. After all, I was just going to pick up our daughter. I had done that before, and it had never resulted in any problem. But let me not get ahead of myself. I'll start at the beginning of the event:

I left my job at around four p.m. Leslie's plane was getting in about six-thirty p.m. I had to consider that I would be running into the rush hour, so I allowed an extra hour in the event that I would run into any traffic jams. The thought of drinking popped into my head a couple of times during the day, but that was all. I hadn't made any plans to drink. As a matter-of-fact, I really wanted to get the whole trip over early so I would be home before it got too late.

As I pulled onto the highway, I suddenly thought it would be nice to pick up a little half-pint of rum. I had gone past only one exit, and I knew there was a liquor store not far from the next exit. I pulled off the highway and picked up the half-pint and was back on the highway without losing too much time. I opened the bottle and wedged it between the bucket seats. The traffic was rather heavy, so I had to be careful. I didn't want to be seen taking a quick nip by another driver. I checked the left lane and through the side mirror, checked the rear mirror, and turned my head to check the right lane. When it was clear on all sides, I picked up the bottle and took a long hard swallow. With my mouth full of rum, I screwed the top back on first and then swallowed down the rum. I hadn't eaten anything, so it wasn't long before the rum started taking effect on me. By the time I got to the New York tollbooth, I had finished the bottle. The rush hour was at its peak, and I had to be extra careful not to get into any accidents. I put up the extra caution sign in my head. I was always able to do that successfully when I was slightly drunk—but only slightly. I had a way of checking myself out. I would look at the lines that divided the lanes. If I saw one line, I was all right. If I saw them double, I knew I shouldn't be driving, but I drove on anyway. I had learned that if I closed one eye, I wouldn't see double, so that's what I did when I was in that condition.

However, on that day I wasn't seeing double, but I was caught in some heavy traffic. It was continual stop and go, and I was starting to worry that I was going to be late. The traffic got even worse, and I was really worried now because I had lost a lot of time. I could see that I wasn't going to make it. I just hoped she didn't worry.

Finally, the traffic opened up, and I was moving again. By the time I got to the airport, her plane had already landed, but I was only about five or ten minutes late. I was surprised to see that the driveway in front of the terminal was practically empty.

I didn't see anyone directing traffic, so I parked directly in front of the door and ran inside. I had hoped to find Leslie right away so I wouldn't leave the car there long. It took longer than I had expected. By the time we got back to where I had left the car, it was not there.

Leslie sensed that I had been drinking and seemed to be upset with me. I asked one of the baggage men if he has seen my car being towed.

"No," he told me. "I've been here all the time, and I'm sure that no car was towed."

He sounded so sure that I began to question myself about where I parked the car. I was in such a hurry that maybe I parked it in the parking lot. I just couldn't remember for sure. I told Leslie to wait so I could go out and look in the lot. Well, let me tell you, it took me about two hours to check out the entire parking lot, and still, I could not find the car.

When I came back to the terminal, I found Leslie sleeping where I had left her. I woke her and told her that the car must have been towed because I couldn't find it anywhere in the parking lot. She was now very upset with me. I finally put her on a limousine going to New Haven and stayed at the airport to attempt to solve the mystery of the missing car.

I needed a place to sit down and try to figure this whole thing out. Naturally I looked for the bar. To find it, I had to walk upstairs. To my disappointment, it was closed when I got there.

I was walking around with my hands in my pockets, trying to figure out my next move. My legs were bothering me from all the walking I had done in the parking lot. I found a spot to sit, and as I was looking at those TV monitors that tell you the flight schedule, I was thinking of how I could get something to drink. After a short while, I once again got up. I walked over and was watching the cars as they were leaving the terminal. I turned my head and glanced in the direction the cars were coming from. There were a few cabs and a couple of cars parked in front of the main entrance. The cabs were dropping off and picking up people. It wasn't until I turned to look the other way again that I realized one of the cars was mine. I turned back to look again and almost jumped with joy.

Sitting right in front of the entrance looking twice its size was my car.

I took my hands out of my pockets and, almost running, reached the front doors. There, right where I had left it was my car. If I had been alone, I think I would have kissed it right on the license plate. Realizing there were people around me, I very casually took out my keys, opened the door, got in, and started the engine. I drove off just as if nothing had happened.

As I drove across the Triboro Bridge, I decided to go to a bar and have a couple of drinks before going back to New Haven. There was a place on 125th Street where I used to play. I decided to go there since it was only a few minutes from the bridge. I parked the car outside and made sure to remember where I parked it this time. I went into the bar and ordered a rum and coke. The place was almost empty except for a few people who looked as though they were friends with the bartender.

As I sipped on my drink, I thought of what had happened at the airport. Apparently, I didn't realize that I had parked the car on the upper level. Between my haste and my drinking, I couldn't figure that out. It was funny when I thought about it, but it was more tragic than funny. I looked at what was happening to me. I was becoming a drunken mess.

I turned on my stool to view the bar and saw that nothing had changed. It still looked the same as it did when I used to come here with my band to play. I picked up my drink and walked over to the side where the bandstand was. I looked at all the empty tables and the empty bandstand. It had been about five years since I played there, but it all looked the same.

I went back to the bar and ordered another drink. The bartender poured the drink, looked at his watch, and said he was closing in about ten minutes. I finished my drink in two minutes and left.

I got in the car, still wanting to do more drinking. I drove awhile until I found another bar on Lenox Avenue. The drinks cost a lot less, and it didn't appear that they were going to close anytime soon. I continued to drink for another two hours. Most of that time I spent talking to the guy on the stool next to me. We talked about a thousand things that had to do with nothing. We kept interrupting each other, always changing the conversation. I guess we were both there doing the same thing. If we were sober, we wouldn't have had anything to say to each other. That's the way it went until closing time. When we left the bar, he went in one direction, and I went in the other. If my life depended on it, I couldn't remember what the guy boked like.

I jumped into my car and headed for New Haven. I had to drive with one eye closed, because this time I had double vision. Even then was having trouble so I pulled off the highway, found a spot to park, and lay down in the rear seat. I must have slept for about three or four hours.

When I opened my eyes, it was already daylight. I jumped up and looked around, trying to figure out where I was. Most of the cars had New York license plates so I new I still had a long way to go. I looked at my watch, and it was just past 8:30 a.m. just down the street I saw The entrance back to the highway. I started the car, made a U-turn, and was back on the highway to New Haven.

I thought of how I was going to explain all this to Nellie. I was sure that by now Leslie had told her I had been drinking and I would have lot of explaining to do.

At this point you would think that I would have had enough, right? Wrong! It was Friday. Not only that, it was the first day of work I had missed all year.

I looked up and saw a sign on the highway reading "Welcome to Connecticut." It was just past nine a.m. I approached the tollbooths, and after I paid my toll, I got off at the next exit to find a liquor store drove around for only a few minutes before I found one. I parked outside and went in to get another half-pint. They didn't have what I wanted in half-pints, so I bought a pint. Then I drove down a couple of locks and turned onto a side street. I parked the car and took a good swallow from the bottle. Within a couple of minutes, I took another, That was the last thing I could remember.

How I managed to drive back to New Haven will always remain a mystery to me. I have only short flashes of the things that happened, but that was after I got back to New Haven. I don't remember what I was thinking when I drove past my house and the schoolyard across the street. I just knew I had to urinate, so I did.

The police were called, and I ended up in the emergency room at the local hospital. That's when my memory started to return.

I don't know how long I was sitting in the waiting room. When I realized what was happening, I just got up and walked out. I didn't have on any shoes, but I didn't let that stop me. It was about a half mile to my house, and I walked it without shoes.

When I walked into the house, I still couldn't think right. I must have had some fear that the police might come and get me because instead of going to bed, I lay down in the closet and closed the door behind me and fell asleep.

By the time Nellie got home, I was fast asleep in the closet. When she didn't see me at home, she panicked. She called my job to see if they knew where I was. Dominic, one of the counselors, came over to the house to help locate me. After a while they found me in the closet. At that point I must have gotten up and thrown myself on the bed.

I slept for a few more hours before I felt Nellie trying to wake me up. I opened my eyes and saw things much clearer. I had slept off the drunk.

Nellie told me that Willie and Edith had come by to see me. I tried not to show it, but I became very upset that they were there to see me. I knew what they were going to tell me. It's what all alcoholics don't want to hear.

I turned to Nellie and asked gruffly, "Why did you have to call them?"

She gave me no answer.

I went into the bathroom to wash up. I would have stayed in the bathroom all night if I thought they would go away. But that would have been ridiculous. I washed my face and brushed my teeth. When I saw myself in the mirror, I couldn't believe it was me. I looked terrible. My face was swollen, and my eyes were bloodshot and puffy. What a terrible sight I was. Now I felt even worse about talking to someone.

It took a lot for me to leave that bathroom, but finally I did. When I walked into the kitchen, I could feel the tension building up inside me.

As I see it now, it was the only way. Someone had to confront me, and this confrontation had to come from people who really cared about me; people who knew what they were doing.

At that point, there was no one better suited than Nellie, Willie, and Edith. It was the first time I could openly admit that I was an alcoholic.

I wasn't ready to do everything we talked about. For example, I didn't think I needed to go into detox. I was certain I wouldn't go through anything physical. The next thing was going to AA. I resisted that because I just wasn't ready to go that far. Willie told me that he would even go to AA meetings with me. I told him I would think about it. Although it appeared that not much was accomplished, one very important thing came out: for the first time I had admitted I was an alcoholic.

As I said before, the first of the twelve steps of Alcoholics Anonymous is: "We admitted we were powerless over alcohol, that our lived had become unmanageable."

XX

I HAD REACHED BOTTOM. AS BAD AS that whole episode was, it was the only way I was going to realize how serious my problem was. The following weekend was the first in a lot of years that I didn't drink. Even though I didn't drink, it wasn't for the right reason. After all I had gone through, I would have to have been totally out of my mind to even think of drinking again. That's the way I was feeling. I had openly made a promise to Nellie that I was not going to drink anymore. And I meant every word of it. I just stayed home for the weekend, getting myself together. I knew I had to go to work and face my staff on Monday, and that wasn't going to be easy.

Then I realized that by now they must know what had happened. They already knew that I drank a lot, but this was more serious than that. They never knew me to miss a day of work because I was so drunk.

This time I didn't just drink and go to bed like I usually did. The one staff member who saw me most was Ana. Nellie and I would often go out with Ana and her husband. She knew that I drank more than the average person, and she would get on me for that. I expected the worst from her.

When I got in Monday morning, no one said a thing about the incident. I could sense that some staff members wanted to talk to me about it, but I guessed it would not be the easiest thing to talk to your boss about.

After my first day back had passed, the tension diminished. By the end of the week, it was much better. I wasn't so lucky with Ana. She got on me real heavy. She would come into my office and close the door behind her. She would even check me out on the weekends. Between her and Edith, I wasn't going to forget the incident very easily. And that was good. They both helped me in different ways. For that I will be eternally grateful.

The weeks became months, and I still kept away from the booze. It was difficult at times, but I managed to stay sober. Deep down inside I still wanted to drink, but I kept reminding myself of what had happened to me in October, and I would cancel out the idea.

Six months passed, and I was still hanging in there, but now the cancellation was becoming postponement. Finally, the postponement started to become plans. As this whole process took place in my mind.

I could feel some anger. I was angry because I couldn't drink like other people. I didn't realize it at the time, but I was even becoming angry at Nellie. I was angry because she wouldn't accept my drinking. She wouldn't accept that I could be a social drinker.

I started looking back at the incident, as it was, just an incident. An accident that just happened that one time. It didn't necessarily mean that I was an alcoholic. Why did I ever say that I was an alcoholic? I didn't really have to say that. If I controlled myself, I could have avoided having that happen to me.

Even though I started thinking this way, I still didn't drink. But I was planning to. I was going to prove once and for all that I could drink. I was not an alcoholic.

At first, I would have an occasional beer, and it didn't lead to anything more. I started having a few rum and Cokes, and even that didn't get out of hand. A year went by, and I was still doing okay. I had even gotten drunk a few times but was not doing things I had been doing in the past. I was trying to prove to everyone that I could drink. I was drinking and getting away with it. No incidents. At least no incidents that anyone could see.

I found that the drinking was starting to increase. I began to worry about it. The Christmas holidays were not far away. Christmas and New Years were dangerous times for anyone who was trying not to drink, so I decided that I was once again going to stop. It was in the middle of November 1985, that I decided not to drink again. Once again, I started to see that no matter how I tried, I just couldn't drink responsibly.

If I could say I learned anything from that incident the previous year, it was that I could never allow myself to go through that again. I was really surprised how the holidays went by, and I didn't drink. It even seemed easier than the first time. Maybe the fact that I was an alcoholic was finally starting to sink in.

In the past year, I had gone to a couple of meetings, but only as an observer. I had also attended some NA meetings, and even though I went for a different reason, I must admit that I was affected by the concept. The people there had no trouble admitting their disease.

I left those meetings wishing I could go back, but I just couldn't bring myself to do it. I had heard at one of the meetings that it was necessary to go to ninety meetings within ninety days. How could I do that? How could I go to a meeting every day? How could I confess to others that I was an alcoholic?

In a way I wanted to do it. I wanted to let go of that pride that was holding me back, but it was extremely difficult for a number of reasons, the main reason being that I was the director of a drug treatment program. What would people think of me? What would they say? Would I lose the respect that I had? And what about my staff—how would they look at me? All these thoughts were running around in my head. I wondered if the people who were members of AA had the same thoughts as I did. Judging from the few meetings that I went to; they certainly didn't appear to.

I also wondered how they were able to take the first step. That seemed to be the hardest part. I just didn't have the nerve to walk into a meeting on my own. I had probably gone to five or six AA and NA meetings in the past, but that was different. I had gone for other reasons other than for myself. I felt as though I were stranded on an island just twenty feet from shore. So close that I could see everything that was going on, but so far away because I was afraid of the water.

It had now been fifteen months since I stopped drinking.

Although I didn't stay completely sober, I was hanging in there, especially during the last two months. But something seemed to be missing. Something was just not there. There was a void that I was always trying to fill.

That feeling was not new to me. It was always there as far back as I could remember. I had very often thought about that and how it affected my life. As much as I tried to get rid of that feeling, I was never successful. Was it something that I alone felt, or did all addicts feel it? Maybe every human on earth felt it, but every human on earth was not an addict. I didn't know. I still don't.

Over the years I have heard and read different theories about this feeling. None have completely convinced me. It's something that I have to look further into myself. Maybe I'll never know, but it just can't end like this.

It was just about the last week in January when I finally entered through the doors of AA. January 28, 1986, to be exact. I can't actually take credit for having become that brave. Someone whom I was very concerned about asked me if I could help them. That person had lost control of their drinking and wanted to try to stop. I volunteered to take the person to AA. I picked up the person, took her to the AA meeting, and then took her home. It went on like that for over a month. On some nights when she didn't feel like going, I went by myself. I found a different meeting to go to every night. Sometimes I went to NA groups. It didn't matter much if I went to AA or

NA; I always got something out of it. I would come home from the meetings feeling good.

The meetings not only helped me with my addiction, but also in a lot of other ways. There were no guarantees that I would never drink again. Right now I could put this pencil down and go have a drink. I could wait until Friday, buy a bottle of rum, and drink away the weekend. I have that choice, but I choose not to drink. I had that same choice twenty-two years ago when I chose not to use heroin again. About ten years later I chose to pick up a drink. Now at age fifty, I realize that I will be a drug addict and an alcoholic all my life. I can't change that, but like I just said, today I have a choice.

I'm not so angry anymore, but I can become angry, and that's okay. I'm not angry at Nellie because she didn't accept my drinking, but we can become angry at each other. As a matter of fact, she can sometimes be a big pain in the exit. But that doesn't take away from the fact that I love her more today than I did in all the years we have shared. I sometimes wonder if she would ever consider writing about her side of our experience.

Well, I think I've said what I had to say. I would like to say more, but then I can't predict the future. Today I am feeling grateful that I didn't take any substance to get high on. Tonight, I will be going to my AA meeting. Tomorrow I'll probably go to my NA meeting.

If I feel like sharing a feeling or a thought in tonight's meeting, I'll just simply raise my hand and say, "Hello, my name Is Bobby Miguel and I'm a drug addict and an alcoholic."

www.ingramcontent.com/pod-product-compliance
Lightning Source LLC
LaVergne TN
LVHW021803060526
838201LV00058B/3215